D0324276

LANGUAGES IN CONFLICT

Richard J. Joy

Published by the Author

If not available from your bookseller, additional copies of this book may be obtained by writing to the Author, c/o:

P.O. Box 2402
Station D
Ottawa, Canada

Money orders should be made payable to R. J. Joy; the price, $6.00 per copy, includes postage in Canada,

Table of Contents

Index to Statistical Tables

Page

Page

Introduction

This book presents the linguistic history of Canada, as revealed by the census records. The basic theme is the conflict between the French and English languages, a conflict which began over two centuries ago and which has had a profound effect on the political and economic development of our country.

Although statistics — almost 70 tables — are the backbone of this work, the bare figures have been fleshed out by inclusion of explanatory material and historical notes, so that the text may be of value to even those readers who are not familiar with the Canadian background.

The first half of the book discusses the various factors influencing the language picture and one chapter is devoted to each of such subjects as Migration, Birth Rates, Assimilation, etc. In the second half, the chapters are arranged along geographical lines, each one presenting the linguistic history of a specific region.

Through the census figures, we can follow the outward movement of French-Canadians from their old parishes along the St. Lawrence, a movement facilitated by the concurrent departure of many persons of British origins from those areas of Quebec Province and of Eastern Ontario which had been originally settled by English-speaking families.

During the third quarter of the 19th Century, the advance guards of this outward movement had established parishes even on the shores of the Pacific and there was a brief period during which the French language appeared to be securing permanent footholds in almost all parts of Canada.

From the figures of the census, however, it is evident that a long-term trend had begun before the end of that century, as the great southward exodus drained the vitality of Canada's French-speaking population and left the Prairies to be occupied by families of other origins.

Today, the English language has unquestioned dominance in the Western Provinces, in Southern Ontario and in the Atlantic Region. Both languages are in more-or-less common use within a "Bilingual Belt" along the Quebec border but the interior of that province is solidly French-speaking.

Although the future is unpredictable, the historical trend has been toward the emergence of a French Canada with increasingly-well-defined boundaries, as the minority islands fade away on both sides of the linguistic frontier.

The conclusions presented in this book are the author's. For the benefit of readers who may wish to do further research, an appendix has been provided which shows the sources of the figures used in the various tables.

Before passing on to the text, a personal note is in order. Although English is the author's mother tongue, the fore-runner of this book was a paper presented in French during the 1962 meeting of l'Association canadienne-française pour l'avancement des sciences. Conflict between the two languages does not prevent French- and English-speaking Canadians from working together and maintaining cordial personal relationships; this book could never have been completed without the assistance and encouragement of friends of both language groups.

Richard J. Joy

Ottawa,
November, 1967.

CHAPTER I

One Hundred Years

One hundred years ago, Canada was just on the verge of nationhood, as the British colonies in North America prepared to merge into one Dominion that would stretch "from sea to sea and from the river to the end of the earth".

In an area as large as that of the United States were to be found only three million people. The high degree of dispersion of the population and the relative isolation of the rural areas, in particular, had meant that each little community could retain the language of its founders; English, French, German and Gaelic were all in current use and the new country was a linguistic checkerboard.

During the past century, however, and despite the temporary importance of other tongues during periods of heavy immigration, two languages have asserted their preeminence. Today, although two-and-a-half million Canadians are of other mother tongues, only English and French can be seriously considered as "languages of Canada".

Until 1867, Ontario and Quebec (as they are now known) were one province and the growth of the relative numerical strength of the British-origin population was an increasing worry to the French-Canadians. As confederation was accompanied by a split between the predominantly-French Quebec and the overwhelmingly-English Ontario, with each of the new provinces free to establish its own school laws, the majority of French-Canadians were, thenceforth, assured of receiving an education in schools of their own language supported by taxes levied by a legislature in which representatives of their own group would hold control. This has been the greatest single factor acting to preserve the French language in North America.

The very fact that control of the provincial legislature (and, thereby, of the school laws) would rest with the French-speaking population of Quebec and with the English-speaking populations of the other provinces, automatically created more-or-less unhappy situations with regard to the educational facilities available to the minority groups. Until recently, however, economic factors have been such that the discomfort suffered by the English-speaking minority in Quebec was relatively slight.

At the time of Confederation, over one-fifth of Quebec's population was of British origin, including half the citizens of Montreal, and this was by far the most important minority, in terms of numbers as well as of wealth and prestige, to be found anywhere within what is today Canada.

However, the French-speaking minorities elsewhere were hardly negligible. Down East, Acadians made up over 8% of the population of Nova Scotia and almost 10% of that of Prince Edward Island, while recent arrivals from the Magdalen Islands had reinforced the French-speaking settlements along the West Coast of Newfoundland. Only in New Brunswick could it be said that the French language had less relative importance in the mid-19th Century than it has today.

In Ontario, the descendants of those who had founded Detroit were still strong in the Essex Peninsula while the Ottawa Valley boasted a French-speaking bishop as evidence of the extent to which those of his language group had acquired a majority position among the Catholics of what was to become our national capital, a superiority which assured the position of French-language instruction in the schools of Eastern Ontario.

In the West, uncounted thousands of Indians and Métis had learned the French language at missionary schools while bishops from the Great Lakes to the shores of the Pacific prepared parishes in eager anticipation of a flood of westward migration from the overcrowded rural areas of Quebec, areas in which the recruiting agents of Archbishop Taché were to work with the zeal of missionaries. Even in 1870, when the West became part of Canada, there seemed little reason to doubt that French would continue to be an important language on the Prairies; Article 23 of the Manitoba Act gave to the French-speaking inhabitants of that new province the same rights as were possessed by the English-speaking minority in Quebec.

Today, however, the linguistic picture in Canada is far different from that described above. As the following chapters will show, linguistic segregation is increasing at an accelerating rate, with the English-speaking population of Quebec fading away (except at Montreal) and the French language hardly ever heard outside an area bounded on the west by a line drawn from Sault Ste. Marie through Ottawa to Cornwall and on the east by a line from Edmundston to Moncton.

The map immediately following this chapter clearly shows that the areas of Ontario and New Brunswick in which French is still in common use are merely the westerly and easterly extensions of Quebec Province. Reference to this map will establish the geography of the Soo-Moncton area, to which frequent reference will be made in this and in subsequent chapters.

Within this Soo-Moncton area live 93% of all Canadians of French mother tongue and, probably, at least 95% of all those who still use French as the language of the home. Elsewhere in Canada, among a total population of almost twelve million, only 560,000 persons (1961 Census) claimed to be able to speak French, including the many for whom it was merely a second or third language.

By way of contrast, consider that part of Quebec Province lying north and east of Montreal. Here, in the heartland of French Canada, 98% of the population speaks French and this region is only slightly less unilingual than are, in the other sense, the Western Provinces, Southern Ontario and the Atlantic Region.

The pattern so common during the 19th Century, of English- and French-speaking communities intermingled within the same geographical region, is now found only along the borders of Quebec Province, within a zone of transition separating French Canada from the English-speaking continent. This "Bilingual Belt" includes Northern Ontario, the Ottawa Valley, Montreal, the Eastern Townships of Quebec and the northern counties of New Brunswick.

It is difficult to believe that the trend toward linguistic segregation can be reversed by mere legislation, even if this be as extensive as some of the recent proposals made by politicians whose sincerity cannot be questioned.

QUEBEC
ST. BONIFACE
SAULT
STE MARIE
MONCTON
YARMOUTH
WINDSOR
FALL RIVER

The map on the opposite page illustrates the extent to which the French-speaking areas of Ontario and of New Brunswick are merely the westerly and easterly extensions of Quebec Province. It shows, also, the extreme isolation, from French Canada, of St. Boniface (Manitoba), Windsor (Ontario), Yarmouth (Nova Scotia) and Fall River (Mass.), all of which were once important centres of French-speaking communities.

Shown with vertical hatching are the eleven counties of Ontario and the seven counties of New Brunswick in which French is spoken by a substantial proportion of the population. Also shown, with horizontal hatching, are the two counties of Quebec (Brome and Pontiac) in which English was still the majority language at the time of the 1961 Census.

CHAPTER II

Bilingual Country, Unilingual Citizens

An extremely significant finding of the 1961 Census was that only 31% of the population of Canada claimed to be able to speak French, even after taking into account all those for whom it was merely a second or third language; this was hardly more than the 30% who reported their ethnic origin as being French. In sharp contrast, 80% of the population could speak English, almost double the number classed by the Census as being of British origin.

The lack of interest shown in the French language by most Canadians of other origins has become a matter of grave concern to French-Canadians and is, at present, the subject of enquiry of a royal commission; the testimony heard by this commission has shown that there is a very wide variety of opinion as to the extent to which the French language should be used in Canada.

The British North America Act of 1867, often referred to as Canada's "constitution", is almost completely silent on the language question. Although Section 133 (which states that either French or English may be used by any person in the debates of the Parliament of Canada or of the Legislature of Quebec or before any court of Canada or of Quebec) has, in recent years, often been cited by French-Canadians as authority for the use of the French language outside Quebec, it is more likely that the prime purpose of this section was to protect the then-existing rights of the English-speaking minority in French-dominated Quebec; section 133 was, actually, invoked for this purpose in 1937, when Duplessis attempted to subordinate the English text of the Statutes of Quebec.

Regardless of the legalities, however, the fact is that English has been the favored language in Canada since 1760. Although some of the earlier British governors were quite sympathetic toward their "Canadiens", economic power has always rested with the predominantly-English-speaking merchant class. This not only set the language to be used at work, but also meant that those educational facilities available to the majority of young

French-Canadians would, for lack of adequate financial support, usually be distinctly inferior to those available to English-speaking children.

Generally speaking, and this applies in Quebec as well as in the other provinces, the educational system of French Canada has been oriented toward instruction of only a very small "élite"; the sons of the wealthy and a few others whose tuition was paid by the Church were able to reach university level but the typical French-speaking child from rural Quebec had, until quite recently, no greater opportunity to study in his own language than had his cousins living in one of the predominantly-French counties of Eastern Ontario.

Throughout French Canada, the responsibility for secondary education has, almost invariably, been entrusted to privately-operated "collèges classiques", rather than to state-run high schools. Even within Quebec, it was rare for tax-supported schools to offer education in French beyond the sixth grade and Articles 2 to 9 of the 1960 Liberal election program deplored the historical fact that very few students from rural and working-class families had been able to attend the French-language universities of Quebec.

For those fortunate enough to receive university education, a knowledge of French alone would not suffice. Just as familiarity with Latin was a prerequisite for those wishing to study for the priesthood and certain liberal professions, so, too, was English essential for all those who wished to obtain degrees in Commerce or Engineering. Figures published in 1961 by "Le Quartier Latin" (newspaper of the students of the Université de Montréal) showed that 70% of the textbooks used in the final year of Business Administration were in English; for Engineering, the figure was 95%.

The fact that a knowledge of English has been a prerequisite for material gain is admitted by even those who ardently favor the French language. To quote the deputy minister of Quebec's Cultural Affairs department: "D'une part, donc, les Canadiens français ont faim et soif de culture française. D'autre part, ils vivent, collectivement, dans des conditions propres à occasionner une dissociation entre leurs aspirations culturelles et les nécessités matérielles au sein desquelles leur existence se poursuit."*

As an indication of the extent to which French has only recently begun to acquire a certain status in Canada, it might be recalled that even the provincial civil service of Quebec used English as the language of work during the 19th Century. The public utilities of Quebec became bilingual only after a vigorous campaign by the young French-Canadian nationalists of the day, in 1910, and most private industry still uses English as the major

*Guy Frégault, speech delivered at Montreal, October First, 1963.

(if not the sole) language of internal communication. Outside Quebec, of course, French would hardly ever be used in factories or offices.

Under these circumstances, and taking into account the North American environment, English is, without question, of so much greater economic value than any other language that it is hardly surprising that very few Canadians can speak French unless they have French ancestors or have lived in a community that was predominantly French-speaking.

(It might be well to remark, before proceeding further, that figures are published, showing the number of persons of each of the various non-French origins having French as their mother tongue. These figures have little practical significance, since any given individual may have seven French great-grandparents yet be classed as "of British origin" if the eighth came from the U.K. or Ireland and stands in the male line of ascent.Use of bulk figures, as below, minimizes this problem.)

Table 1

Number of Persons claiming ability to speak French vs. Number of French ethnic origin, by Regions of the country, 1961 Census

Geographical Region	*of French Origin*	*Able to Speak French*	*Ratio*
Atlantic	147,000	82,000	56%
Northern N.B.	208,000	210,000	101%
Interior Quebec	2,119,000	2,177,000	103%
S. & W. Quebec	2,122,000	2,417,000	114%
E. & N. Ontario	366,000	358,000	98%
Southern Ontario	282,000	230,000	82%
Western Provinces	296,000	247,000	83%
Canada	5,540,000	5,721,000	103%

As can be seen from the figures of the above table, those who speak French (including all those for whom it is merely a second or third language) are less numerous than those of French origin, in every region in which English is the majority language.

The following table looks at another aspect of the language question. City-dwelling adult males are the most bilingual segment of Canada's population, yet even these are seldom capable of expressing themselves in both of Canada's "official" languages.

Table 2

Percentages of Adult Males speaking English Only, English & French and French Only, in various Canadian Cities, 1961 Census

City	*English Only*	*English & French*	*French Only*
St. John's	98%	2%	—%
Halifax	91	9	—
Saint John	89	11	—
Moncton	64	35	1
Quebec	1	46	53
Montreal	20	59	19
Ottawa/Hull	54	41	4
Sudbury	66	32	1
Toronto	92	6	—
Windsor	83	16	1
Winnipeg	90	9	—
Edmonton	92	7	—
Vancouver	93	6	—
Victoria	94	5	—

Totals are less than 100% in some cases due to presence of persons who speak neither English nor French.

In each of the cities outside Quebec Province where thele is any significant degree of bilingualism, it will be found that this is attributable to the presence of French-Canadian minorities. Those whose mother tongue was French made up over 31% of the adult male population of Moncton, over 36% at Ottawa/Hull, 29% at Sudbury and 13% at Windsor; the low degree of bilingualism among those of other mother tongues is particularly remarkable (a French-Canadian might say "shocking") in these four cities, where there would appear to be a substantial contact between the two language groups.

Ottawa and Quebec are the capitals, respectively, of a bilingual country and of a bilingual province, yet, in each, fewer than half the adult male citizens claimed to be able to speak both languages. Only at Montreal did the two languages have approximately equal status and only there did the majority ot the adult male population call itself bilingual.

For the population as a whole, bilingualism has been declining in recent decades. It is difficult to say whether this is part of a long term trend, since three non-recurring factors must be taken into account: Newfoundland's entry into the statistics in 1951, the postwar surge of immigrants and the higher proportion of children among the recent population.

Table 3

Percentages of Canadian Population speaking English Only, English & French and French Only, at the last four censuses

	1931	*1941*	*1951*	*1961*
English Only	67.5%	67.2%	67.0%	67.4%
English & French	12.7	12.8	12.3	12.2
French Only	17.1	19.0	19.6	19.1
Neither	2.7	1.0	1.1	1.3

Although the figures for the country as a whole may not show any decisive trend, there is no mistaking the trend toward French unilingualism within the Province of Quebec; this is particularly noticeable in the urban areas.

Table 4

Percentages of Adult Males speaking English Only, English & French and French Only, in urban areas of Quebec Province, at the last four censuses

	1931	*1941*	*1951*	*1961*
English Only	19.7%	17.1%	14.0%	13.0%
English & French	58.5	57.2	56.3	52.9
French Only	21.1	25.6	29.3	33.2

Although it may be true that the great majority of those who are bilingual, in the limited sense of being able to speak both English and French, are of French descent, this is due, almost entirely, to environmental factors and does not appear to indicate any special aptitude for languages on the part of French-Canadians. When economic and other incentives are lacking, so, too, is a knowledge of the other language.

In several counties of Quebec, only 5% of the French-speaking population claimed to be bilingual. In New Brunswick, where the law states that English must be taught in the schools, Madawaska and Gloucester Counties reported only 30% bilingualism among those of French mother tongue. Even in Ontario, those who spoke "French Only" were more numerous than those who spoke "English and French" in Russell and Prescott Counties.

All the counties mentioned above are predominantly rural. The next table, therefore, gives figures for selected cities to show the rate at which French-Canadians become bilingual under a variety of environmental conditions.

Table 5

Percentages of males of French mother tongue claiming to be bilingual, by age groups and by city of residence, 1961 Census

Age Group:	*5-9*	*10-14*	*15-19*	*25-34*
City				
Chicoutimi	1%	1%	9%	33%
Shawinigan	1	3	18	44
Quebec City	2	5	23	44
Jacques Cartier	4	9	34	58
Montreal North	5	17	48	66
Hull	12	33	70	84
Cornwall	72	93	97	97
Sudbury	87	97	98	97
Moncton	88	98	97	97
St. Boniface	96	98	99	98

The cities chosen for the above table fall into three distinct categories:

1. Chicoutimi, Shawinigan and Quebec are deep inside French Canada and adolescents have relatively little contact with the English language;

2. Jacques Cartier, Montreal North and Hull are all within the Province of Quebec and their populations are overwhelmingly French-speaking; however, these cities are subject to anglicizing influences from Montreal or Ottawa, where many of their young people expect to seek employment;

3. The last four cities have strong French-speaking minorities but are located outside Quebec Province and the English language dominates in fact as well as in law.

These figures indicate that the French-Canadian living in the interior of Quebec Province will learn English, if at all, only after reaching an age at which he has started to earn his living. On the outskirts of Montreal, there is a greater degree of bilingualism and it commences at an earlier age. At Hull, where there is constant exposure to the English language, the average French-Canadian is bilingual by the time he has left school. Outside Quebec Province, however, a knowledge of English is, generally, acquired before the child has even entered school.

Canadians of English mother tongue react in a similar manner to their environment. The 1961 Census showed 982 persons of English mother tongue, aged 15-19, living in the metropolitan area of Quebec City but it found only 135 persons of this age group who spoke "English Only". Outside Quebec Province, however, very few English-speaking Canadians would bother to learn a language which they will seldom have occasion to use in business or socially.

This factor indicates that bilingualism may be on the decline, despite efforts by the federal government to promote use of French in the civil service. As the minorities fade away (those of English mother tongue from the interior of Quebec, those of French tradition elsewhere), so, too, will our bilingual population tend to disappear, everywhere except within that narrow belt along the Quebec border where both language groups are present in sufficient strength that neither has any immediate possibility of completely displacing the other.

CHAPTER III

The Seven Regions of Canada

The true extent to which the two major language groups in Canada are becoming segregated is seldom fully appreciated. This is, in large part, due to the fact that Census figures are hardly ever discussed other than on the basis of provincial totals.

The sheer size of Canada's political units makes such a basis unreasonable. Although there is practically no similarity between, for example, the town of St. Isidore de Prescott and the metropolitan area of Toronto, the figures for both are bulked together in one total labelled "Ontario".

In New Brunswick, too, there is very little resemblance (linguistically) between the north and the south of the province: in Madawaska, 94% of the county's population gave French as their mother tongue but 98% of the inhabitants of Carleton County spoke "English Only".

The most common misconception, however, is to visualize the typical resident of Quebec Province as a person who, if not himself a French-Canadian, is, at least, constantly exposed to the French language. It is not easy for people in other parts of Canada to appreciate that there are, in metropolitan Montreal, half-a-million people who are living, usually quite comfortably, without any knowledge of the majority tongue of the province in which they happen to find themselves.

We have, therefore, discarded provincial divisions (except in those cases when figures are not available on any other base) and will use in this study a division of the country into seven relatively homogeneous regions. The four Western Provinces will be viewed as one region, as will the four Atlantic Provinces after removal of northern New Brunswick, a region in itself. Quebec and Ontario will each be divided into two regions.

These regions were populated at different times and under greatly different circumstances; it is, therefore, not surprising that they should differ greatly in the ethnic makeups of their populations.

Table 6

Distribution of Ethnic Origins in the various Regions of Canada, 1961 Census

	British	*French*	*German & Dutch*	*Ukrainian*	*Italian*	*Scandinavian*
Atlantic	80%	9%	5%	—%	—%	1%
Northern N.B.	34	62	1	—	—	1
Interior Quebec	3	95	—	—	—	—
S. & W. Quebec	17	70	2	—	4	—
E. & N. Ontario	44	34	6	2	3	1
S. & W. Ontario	63	5	10	2	5	1
West	49	6	15	7	1	6
Canada	44	30	8	3	2	2

Totals are less than 100% in each case due to presence of persons of unlisted origins.

The Atlantic Region includes Newfoundland, which has had an English-speaking population for over three centuries; elsewhere, major immigration began in 1749, with the founding of Halifax. Virtually all the Acadians were cleared out of this region during the latter half of the 18th Century and the present population is overwhelmingly of British stock, the area having become economically unattractive before heavy immigration of Europeans began in the 19th Century. The German/Dutch element dates back to the founding of Lunenburg in 1753.

Excluded from the region we have designated as "Atlantic" are the northern counties of New Brunswick.* Here live the descendants of Acadians evicted from Beaubassin, Annapolis and elsewhere during the 18th Century, plus a few French-Canadians whose ancestors came down through Temiscouata or, more recently, the Matapedia Valley. In the same seven counties will be found Maritimers of British origin who are only half as numerous as the French-speaking population but who have found it completely unnecessary to learn the language of the majority group.

Although there are pockets of English-speaking population in the Gaspé and around Quebec City, most of the interior of Quebec Province, that part lying north and east of Montreal, is solidly French in both origin and language. This is the most homogeneous of our seven regions and is,

*Gloucester, Kent, Madawaska, Northumberland, Restigouche, Victoria and Westmorland.

also, notable for the fact that five out of six of its inhabitants are unable to speak English. As this is an area of high birth rates and of economic underdevelopment, the net emigration from the region is high and has an important role in augmenting the French-speaking populations of other regions.

Quite distinct is the South and West of Quebec Province. In this region are the Eastern Townships, Montreal and the counties of the Ottawa Valley, all of which had English-speaking populations during the early part of the 19th Century and in which the language of the majority has become French only within the past hundred years. This region contains most of the English-speaking population of the province and, for economic as well as historical reasons, the English language still has a very considerable status, being spoken by almost half those whose mother tongue is French. However, the growing importance of the French language has made this the region of Canada in which will be found the greatest number of bilinguals among those of English mother tongue, as also the majority of those immigrants who have assimilated to the French language.

The border between Quebec and Ontario follows a line traced in 1791 along the ethno-linguistic frontier of that time. Since then, however, many tens of thousands of Quebec's excess population have spilled over into Eastern and Northern Ontario and the eleven counties* along the border now have, from a language viewpoint, more resemblance to the counties of Western Quebec than to those of Southern Ontario. For this reason, the area has been treated as a separate region.

The southern part of Ontario, the industrial heart of Canada, has received a great variety of immigrants over the past two centuries but two-thirds of its population is still of British origin, making the region second only to the Atlantic Provinces in this respect. Although the 1961 Census reported some 282,000 persons of French ethnic origin in this region, assimilation has been heavy; among the population as a whole, not one person in twenty can speak French as even a second or third language.

The great expanse of Canada west of the Great Lakes was virtually empty a century ago and those who came to colonize it included many of Central and Eastern European origins. Less than half the present population is of British stock; nevertheless, English is the universal language and French is heard in only a few pockets, such as those around St. Boniface, Gravelbourg and Falher.

Looking at the language picture presented by the 1961 Census, we find that the interior of Quebec Province is solidly French-speaking. Adjacent are three regions in which both languages are in common use:

*Algoma, Carleton, Cochrane, Glengarry, Nipissing, Prescott, Renfrew, Russell, Stormont, Sudbury and Timiskaming.

these constitute a bilingual belt between French Canada and the English-speaking continent. Finally, there are the three regions in the West, South and East of the country in which English is the universal language.

Arranging the seven regions in order, based on the degree to which their respective populations speak French, we have:

1. Interior Quebec — Here over 95% of the population gave French as their mother tongue and only 2% speak "English Only". In this region, French is the universal language although English is still used, to a diminishing extent, in heavy industry and in government services. Those catering to the tourist industry must also be proficient in English.
2. Southern Quebec and the Ottawa Valley — Although 70% of the inhabitants of this region gave French as their mother tongue and although the laws of Quebec provide full tax support to French-language schools, French is understood by less than a third of the minority while English is spoken by perhaps 40% of the majority. Generally speaking, the French language predominates in government and ecclesiastical activities but English is the more important in industry; due to the greater economic benefits, a majority of immigrants assimilate to the English, rather than to the French, language.
3. Northern New Brunswick — In these seven counties, French is the mother tongue of 59% of the population but is spoken by practically none of the minority group and English is the more common language in the region. The birth rate of the Acadians has dropped sharply in recent decades and this group is now losing ground due to massive emigration and, to an increasing extent, through assimilation of those who remain in the province.
4. Eastern and Northern Ontario — In the eleven counties which form a band, along the Quebec border, running from the St. Lawrence River to the Upper Lakes, French is the mother tongue of 30% of the population and has official status in the tax-supported schools. Franco-Ontarians hold many important positions in civil and ecclesiastical government and the 1961 Census indicates that fewer than one-quarter of those of French descent have been assimilated to the majority language.
5. The Atlantic Region — In the four Atlantic Provinces, excepting the northern counties of New Brunswick, the effects of assimilation are very marked. French is now spoken by only 5% of the total population of this region, even after counting those for whom it is merely a

second or third language, and has a local importance only in a few rural areas, such as the Diocese of Yarmouth and the southern part of Cape Breton Island.

6. The Western Provinces — English-speaking settlers came out from Ontario in great numbers during the last quarter of the 19th Century and the later immigrants from Europe assimilated almost entirely to the English language, leaving the few French-speaking Westerners hopelessly outnumbered and able to survive only through the relative isolation of their colonies. The most recent census shows that the younger generation has been two-thirds assimilated and the French-speaking population of the West appears well on the way toward a final disappearance.

7. Southern Ontario — In the industrial heartland of Canada, not one person in forty gave French as his mother tongue in 1961. Although there are some schools in which instruction is given in French, the sentiment of both civil and religious authorities has favored assimilation and four out of five of the younger generation of French ethnics use English as the language of the home.

In the following chapters, we shall discuss the position of the French language, and of those speaking it, on the basis of these seven regions. This will, we believe, enable the reader to obtain a better picture of the extent to which the language boundaries in Canada are hardening, with the consequent elimination of minorities everywhere except within a relatively narrow bilingual belt.

CHAPTER IV

From Moncton to The Soo

In the previous chapter, we discussed the seven regions into which Canada divides on a language basis. In three of these, French is the mother tongue of a majority of the population and in a fourth it is spoken by a sizable minority.

These four regions make up an area 1,000 miles long, bounded on the West by a line drawn from Sault Ste. Marie through Ottawa to Cornwall and on the East by a line from Edmundston to Moncton. Within these limits, French is a language in general use; outside this area, it is rarely heard.

Table 7

Number of Persons speaking French as mother tongue or as minor language, by Regions of the country, 1961 Census

Region	*Total Population*	*Speak French as Mother Tongue*	*Other*
Atlantic	1,561,000	62,000	20,000
Northern N.B.	336,000	199,000	11,000
Interior Quebec	2,227,000	2,137,000	41,000
S. & W. Quebec	3,032,000	2,133,000	283,000
E. & N. Ontario	1,062,000	307,000	51,000
S. Ontario	5,174,000	118,000	112,000
West	4,846,000	167,000	80,000
Canada	18,238,000	5,123,000	598,000

As can be seen from the above table, over 90% of all Canadians who claimed to have a knowledge of the French language were found within the Soo-Moncton limits. Outside this area, not one person in twenty could speak French and not one in forty would use it as the language of the home.

Within the Soo-Moncton area, French is understood by over three-quarters of the population, most of whom use it as the language of their homes, and is heard on the streets and in the shops and factories. Elsewhere, in the Western Provinces, in Southern Ontario and in the Atlantic Region, there are only isolated pockets of French-speakers — Yarmouth, Welland, Windsor, St. Boniface, Gravelbourg and a few others.

How does it happen that the language boundaries have crystallized to such an extent? What forces have interacted to produce this Soo-Moncton line?

In the east, the boundary between the two language groups was established two centuries ago, when the Acadians were evicted from their old homes and pushed up into Madawaska and the counties along the Gulf of St. Lawrence. There has, ever since, been a distinction between the north and south of New Brunswick, only the former having any sizable number of French-speakers.

Elsewhere, however, in the south and west of Quebec Province, the language frontier of even the mid-19th Century had little resemblance to that found today. At every census until 1911, new counties showed French-speaking majorities; due to the high birth rate typical of a rural people, the numbers of the French-Canadians increased so rapidly that they had been able to occupy almost all parts of Quebec by the beginning of the present century and were pushing onward into Eastern and Northern Ontario in what seemed to be an irresistible tide.

However, the great exodus of young people toward the mill towns of New England had subtly sapped the vitality of French Canada. By 1901, just as the waves of European immigration were about to sweep into Canada, the westward movement of the French language had come to a virtual stop* and there were only weak contingents ahead of the line running from Cornwall to Sault Ste. Marie.

The decade 1901-1911 saw some consolidation, with French-speaking majorities appearing in Argenteuil, Stanstead and Restigouche (N.B.) Counties, but the old days of easy outward expansion had passed. The coming of millions of immigrants into Ontario and Western Canada completely changed the picture.

During the 19th Century, the French-Canadians had been advancing virtually without opposition; often, in fact, they were welcomed into new areas by mill-owners seeking low-cost labor or by farmers of the original

*Although several tens of thousands of French-Canadians went West after 1901, their numbers were negligible compared to those of the newcomers from overseas.

British stocks who wished to sell out before moving to the new lands of the West. After 1901, however, they would have to compete for every job and for every acre of land, against newcomers from Europe who would work just as hard as they and who would accept just as low a standard of living.

This competition is particularly evident in the ethnic makeup of the cities along the edge of the Soo-Cornwall region. At Sudbury, the population is divided almost equally into British, French and Others; at Sault Ste. Marie, almost 40% of the citizens are of the "Third Groups" and at the Lakehead those of mixed European origins make up half the population and are ten times as numerous as those of French origin.

Had it not been for the availability of immigrants from Europe, French-Canadians might well have been recruited to fill the industrial jobs in these three cities, as they had been by mill-owners in New England, the Eastern Townships and the Ottawa Valley. The three cities mentioned, as well as many others, would then have become centres of strength, rather than of weakness, for the French language and there would, today, be an unbroken line of communications between Quebec and the French-speaking settlements of the Western Provinces.

Instead, the Europeans came. With very few exceptions, they assimilated to the English language (although, in most cases, retaining their old religions and traditions). They filled up the Prairies and the industrial towns of Ontario. By 1931, when immigration came to a temporary stop, the linguistic frontier had become clearly established.

The French-Canadians, too, were changing. Thanks, in part, to the work of Father Lévesque and others at Laval, they are now demanding wages quite comparable to those paid English-speaking Canadians. Their standards of living have risen and they are no longer willing to listen to those who preach the occupation of marginal farms as the sacred duty of the French race. Thus, there is no longer any reason (of an economic nature) for mill-owners or others to encourage them to come into new areas.

Other social changes have also played their part in discouraging further outward migration. Men may accept working in English but French-Canadian wives have difficulty adjusting to the new environment. Politicians like to stress the need for French-language schools but this is only one small part of the larger problem: without French-speaking neighbors, without French-language newspapers and television, daily life lacks diversion; in the stores, it is difficult to be served in French; if a child falls ill, how often can a doctor be found who will understand symptoms described over the telephone in excited French?

Even half a century ago, it was possible for a few hundred French-

Canadians to form a completely self-contained community, within which all their needs could be satisfied. An example is Maillardville, set up in 1909 to shelter the families of men brought from Hull to British Columbia by the Fraser Mills Lumber Company; as the newcomers bought lots and erected their own houses, the only cost to the company which recruited them was that of the materials contributed toward the building of a church and school.

Today, a company wishing to bring in a French-Canadian work force would be faced with a staggering bill for all the amenities which would be necessary to fully satisfy the requirements of the new workers and of their families; it is unlikely that this initial cost could ever be recouped from savings in labor costs. Thus, it is unlikely that we shall ever again see massive recruiting of the type common during the last century.

As will be described in detail in a later chapter, migration from Quebec has now dwindled to the merest trickle and the French-speaking communities outside the Soo-Moncton limits have become vanishing islands in a steadily-encroaching sea of English-speakers. The grandchildren of those who went West in earlier decades are intermarrying and assimilating; the minorities are fading away as the older generations die off.

The result, as the following table shows, is that those Canadians who still retain the French language are, increasingly, to be found only within the Soo-Moncton limits and, particularly, within the Province of Quebec.

Table 8

Percentage of all Canadians of French mother tongue, living in Quebec and in other parts of Canada, Censuses of 1911, 1941, 1951 and 1961

	1911	*1941*	*1951*	*1961*
Quebec Province	78%	81%	82%	83%
Adjacent Counties of Ontario	6	6½	6	6
Adjacent Counties of New Brunswick	5	4½	4½	4
Outside the Soo-Moncton limits	11	8	7½	7

Even the above figures tell only part of the story. Among those living outside the Soo-Moncton limits and who learned French in infancy, many have, through linguistically-mixed marriage or other circumstances, come to adopt English as the present language of their homes, despite the fact that the census continues to report French as their mother tongue. That English is the language in which they are bringing up their children can be seen from examination of the mother tongues reported for those of the younger age groups; this means, of course, that the disappearance of the French-speaking minorities will accelerate as the older generations, those who came from Quebec and their children, gradually die off.

However, the other side of this picture, the one that should bring some consolation to French-Canadians, is that the perpetuation of the French language seems assured within the Soo-Moncton limits and, in particular, within that part of it which is subject to the school and labor laws of Quebec.

A measure of the strength of a language can be obtained by comparing the numbers of those who speak it with those who are of the relevant ethnic origin. The following table shows that, among the younger generation, three-quarters of those of French descent living outside the Soo-Moncton limits were using English as the language of the home, the language reported for their children.

Table 9

Apparent Assimilation of persons of French origin, living in Quebec and in other parts of Canada, 1961 Census

Region	*Population of French Origin aged 0-4*	*Population of French M. Tongue aged 0-4*	*Apparent Assimilation*
Quebec Province	561,950	563,564	negative
Northern N.B.	30,719	28,376	8%
Northern and Eastern Ontario	54,627	40,089	27%
Western Provinces	43,060	14,412	67%
Atlantic Region	20,588	5,169	75%
Southern Ontario	40,071	8,135	80%

We shall discuss assimilation in considerably more detail in the following chapter. Suffice to say here that the figures of Table 9 point out the essential difference in conditions on the two sides of the Soo-Moncton line. On one side, the French language should be able to survive indefinitely; on the other, the social and economic forces which have already led to the assimilation of three-quarters of those of French origin, among the present younger generation, are too strong to be offset by the mere provision of schools and television programs in the minority language.

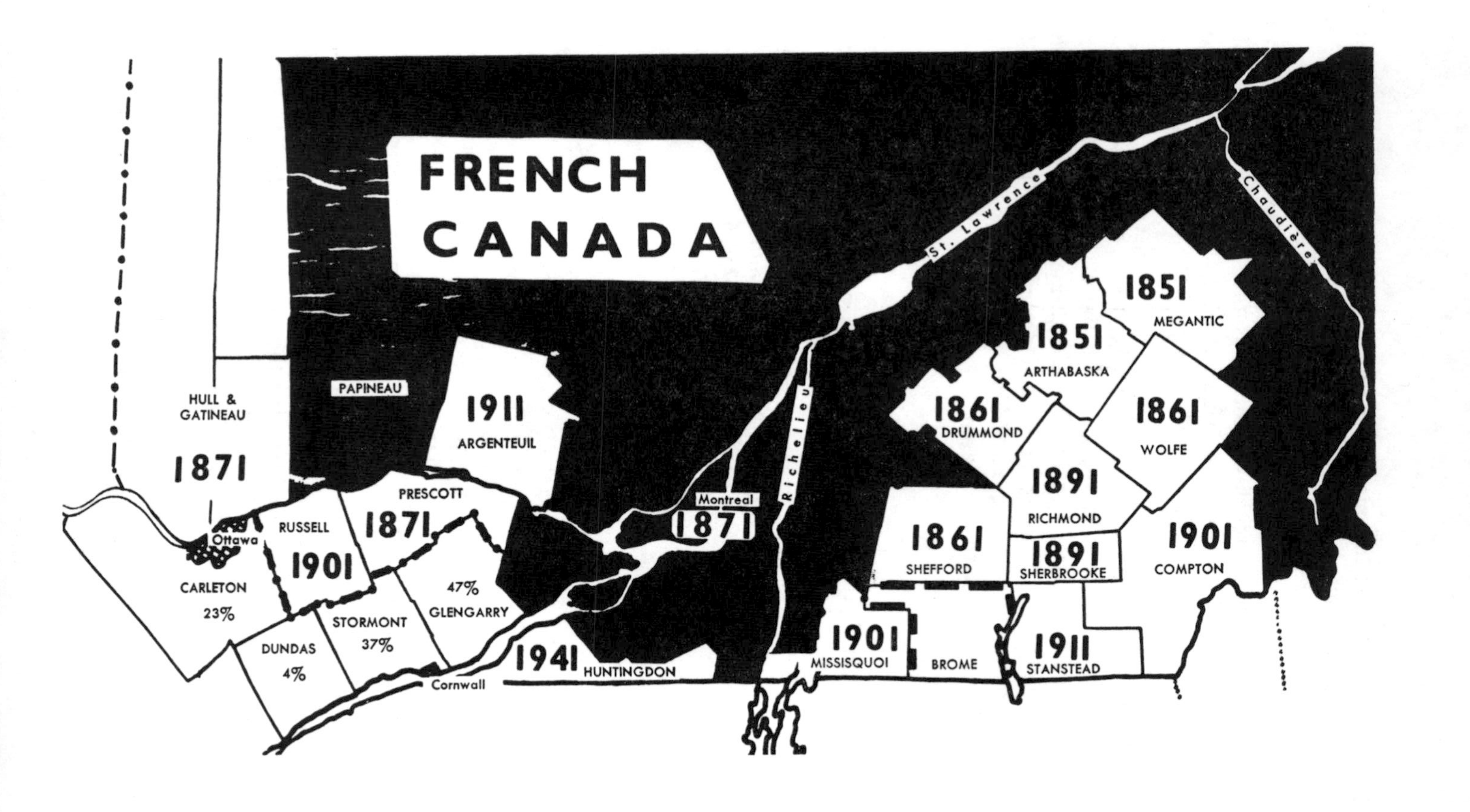
FRENCH CANADA
HULL & GATINEAU
1871
PAPINEAU
1911
ARGENTEUIL
Ottawa
CARLETON
23%
RUSSELL
1901
PRESCOTT
1871
47%
GLENGARRY
STORMONT
37%
DUNDAS
4%
Cornwall
1941
HUNTINGDON
Montreal
1871
St. Lawrence
Richelieu
Chaudière
1851
MEGANTIC
1851
ARTHABASKA
1861
DRUMMOND
1861
WOLFE
1891
RICHMOND
1861
SHEFFORD
1891
SHERBROOKE
1901
COMPTON
1901
MISSISQUOI
BROME
1911
STANSTEAD

The gradual expansion of French Canada into the Eastern Townships and the Ottawa Valley can be followed on the map shown opposite. Areas occupied prior to 1851 are shown in black while the dates in the other counties are those of the first census at which a French majority was reported.

Although Pontiac County (42% French in 1961) in Western Quebec and Glengarry County (47% French) in Eastern Ontario could still follow Huntingdon, which did not show a French-speaking majority until 1941, the western limits of French Canada appear to be, essentially, stabilized; during recent decades, the relative importance of those of French mother tongue has been declining among the population of Carleton County (to less than 23% in 1961) and the Ottawa-Cornwall line appears to be an impenetrable barrier to further expansion of the French-speaking area.

CHAPTER V

Elsewhere, Assimilation

As Professor Brunet has so well stated: "Certains mots qu'utilise l'historien pour décrire les phénomènes sociaux qu'il étudie charrient avec eux une lourde charge d'émotivité. Les passions et les réactions qu'ils soulèvent dans les esprits embrouillent les notions les plus simples."*

The word "assimilation" is, to the more militant French-Canadian, a red flag. To him, it conjures up visions of innocent little children in Saskatchewan being forced to attend English-language schools and, thereby, "losing their heritage". It is, in the French-Canadian press, used only when referring to persons of French origin who now use English as their first language.

However, this aspect of assimilation is a very recent phenomenon. During the late 18th Century and well into the 19th, assimilation in Canada tended to be in the other direction as French expansion engulfed many small colonies of Irish, Scottish and English origin and as French-Canadian families welcomed into their homes the orphans of Irish immigrants. Thousands of Frasers, Ryans, Robertsons, Farrells, Flynns and Johnsons, who now speak only French, are living testimony to the absorptive power of French Canada and, on the very outskirts of the city in which this is written, Hull County in Quebec and Russell County in Ontario each reported that residents of French mother tongue outnumbered those of French origin, in 1961.

If we take the difference between "Ethnic origin French" and "Mother tongue French" as being a measure of assimilation, then a definite pattern stands out from the results of the 1961 Census.

For reporting purposes, Canada is divided into some 250 census divisions. Arranging these into six groups, according to the percentage of persons of French mother tongue among their respective populations, we obtain the figures shown in Table 10.

---

*Michel Brunet: La Présence anglaise et les Canadiens (1958).

Table 10

Number of persons of French mother tongue vs. number of French origin, by groups of Census Divisions, 1961 Census

% of French M.T. in each division	*— French Population — by Origin*	*by M.T.*	*Ratio, M.T./Origin*
95-100	1,558,051	1,569,066	101%
70- 95	1,652,511	1,662,905	101%
50- 70	1,236,055	1,240,096	100%
30- 50	242,840	206,179	85%
5- 30	417,629	283,690	68%
0- 5	433,260	161,215	37%

As the above table shows, the French language has been able to more than hold its own in those parts of the country in which French-speakers are in the majority and has lost ground only slightly in those census divisions where at least 30% of the population is of French mother tongue.

Heavy assimilation is noticeable only in those areas in which the French-speaking population is outnumbered by at least two-to-one and the really massive language loss has been concentrated in those census divisions in which French-Canadians are less than 5% of the total population.

These figures support the belief that it is the social milieu, more than any other single factor, which has determined whether the French language could survive in any given area of the country. That the school laws and other legislation have had only a secondary influence can be demonstrated by making a more detailed examination of the assimilation picture within a single province.

In Ontario, only Prescott and Russell Counties had French-speaking majorities in 1961; in this two-county area, persons of French mother tongue were slightly more numerous than those of French origin.

In the counties of Eastern and Northern Ontario in which French-speakers made up between one-third and one-half of the total population, the mother tongue/ethnic origin ratio ranged between 93% and 77%, indicating that there had been only moderate assimilation by the time of the 1961 Census. These five counties reported 155,000 residents of French mother tongue, only 15% below the number of those of French origin.

It is only in the overwhelmingly-English areas of the province that high assimilation rates can be found. Since the same provincial statutes are in force throughout Ontario, their influence can not have been the primary force toward assimilation.

As will be discussed in greater detail in the next chapter, there are definite gains in precision if we examine only the figures for the youngest age group, rather than those for the population of all ages. The following table, therefore, presents the apparent assimilation found among young persons of French origin living in various parts of Ontario. ("Apparent Assimilation" is the complement of the "Mother Tongue/Ethnic Origin Ratio" we have presented in Table 10.)

Table 11

Apparent Assimilation of persons of French origin,
vs. relative concentration of persons of French mother tongue,
for specified areas of Ontario, 1961 Census

	Population of French M.T. (All ages)		*Apparent Assimilation, 0-4 group*
	Number	*/Total pop.*	
Counties			
Russell & Prescott	38,700	80%	1%
Cochrane	44,100	46%	13%
Glengarry & Stormont	30,300	39%	31%
Nipissing & Sudbury	80,300	34%	28%
Algoma	13,200	12%	52%
Renfrew	5,500	6%	77%
Metro Areas			
Hamilton	6,000	1½%	82%
Toronto	26,000	1½%	83%
Windsor	19,900	*	83%

*Persons of French mother tongue make up 10% of the population of Windsor but would represent only 1 - 2% of the total population of the Windsor-Detroit metropolis.

Table 10 was for all of Canada and presented figures for all age groups, while Table 11 showed only Ontario figures and focussed on assimilation among the younger generation. Both tables, however, support the same conclusions: that the French language has been capable of surviving in those areas in which it is spoken by a majority of the population but that assimilation becomes increasingly severe as the proportion of French-speakers among the total population declines.

The figures of Table 11 bring out a fact that is of major importance when evaluating the chances for survival of those minority groups living outside the Soo-Moncton limits: in the metropolitan areas of Southern Ontario, it would appear that five out of six young adults of French origin are now using English as the language of the home, the language being learned by their children.

Table 12 shows that a high rate of assimilation is characteristic of almost all cities in the predominantly-English parts of Canada. Here, again, it is the social milieu which enters into play, the contact between members of various language groups being more intense in urban than in rural areas.

Table 12

Apparent Assimilation of persons of French origin, by provinces and rural vs. urban, 1961 Census

	Rural Farm	*Rural non-farm*	*Urban*
Newfoundland	98%	93%	95%
P.E.I.	54	59	91
Nova Scotia	44	56	92
New Brunswick	2	8	27
Ontario	28	42	53
Manitoba	20	42	62
Saskatchewan	44	64	83
Alberta	42	70	80
British Columbia	87	90	87
Canada, outside Quebec but including border regions of Ontario and N.B.	30%	39%	58%

Assimilation proceeds through contact. Without the protective shell of the rural French parish, the city-dweller is constantly exposed to the English language. His children will, almost invariably, learn the language of their English-speaking playmates and a high proportion of the French-origin adolescents will find themselves marrying partners who are of the majority group; children of such couples may be able to understand both parents but would seldom choose French as their major language.

It should be noted, in passing, that language and religion are far from being synonymous and that abandonment of the French language does not, in itself, bring about any change in the church attended. Among the 1,299,000 persons of French origin living outside Quebec in 1961, there were 1,112,000 Catholics although only 801,000 of French mother tongue. Since, outside the Soo-Moncton limits, only one Catholic in nine is of French mother tongue, many linguistically-mixed marriages are contracted with fellow-parishioners.

Having examined, in the previous pages, the situation revealed by the 1961 Census, let us now look at the historical background, as shown by the figures of the three previous censuses. Table 13 is calculated in the same way as were Tables 11 and 12, using the Ethnic Origin and Mother Tongue figures for the youngest age group.

Table 13

Apparent Assimilation of persons of French origin, by provinces, Censuses of 1931-1961

	1931	*1941**	*1951*	*1961*
Newfoundland	n.a.	n.a.	91%	94%
P.E.I.	30%	37%	62	68
Nova Scotia	40	51	62	73
New Brunswick	3	4	9	14
Ontario	31	26	40	49
Manitoba	12	6	33	49
Saskatchewan	21	23	49	65
Alberta	33	37	57	70
British Columbia	70	76	83	88
Canada, outside Quebec	20%	23%	38%	49%

*The seeming recovery in 1941, particularly in Manitoba, is attributable to rewording of two census questions, and does not represent a reversal of the trend.

If the border regions of Ontario and New Brunswick be removed from the above totals, then the apparent assimilation outside the Soo-Moncton limits was just over 73% in 1961. In other words, three out of four young adults of French ethnic origin are now using the English language in their homes; in 1931, the proportion had been only one in three.

Over this period of just thirty years, the proportion of French ethnics retaining their language in P.E.I. and Nova Scotia has dropped from 62% to 28%; in the four Western Provinces, the drop has been from 76% to

33%. It is not merely coincidental that these three decades have seen the universal introduction of radio and television into the home and, possibly even more important, the rise of highway transportation which has almost destroyed the former isolation of those living in rural communities.

While the forces favoring assimilation have been increasing, sociological and economic factors have been enfeebling the resistance of the minority groups. Schools, radio stations and newspapers have become much more expensive than previously but the French-speaking communities are often without financial resources: in Nova Scotia, for example, half of those who have retained the French language are living in three rural counties where the average income is under $2,100 per year and, in New Brunswick, the newspaper of the Acadians has been kept alive only through cash subsidies from the government of Quebec.

Also, there tends to be a selective down-grading of the educational level of the minorities, through emigration and assimilation of those who should be the leaders of tomorrow. Studies made by graduate students of Laval University in 1950 showed that those who remained in their rural county were, typically, less educated than those who migrated to the cities. Superimposed upon this is another factor affecting those from outside the Soo-Moncton limits who are of university calibre: if they wish to study in French, they must leave their homes and spend several years at Ottawa, Moncton or one of the Quebec universities. Once they have seen the much greater opportunities available within Quebec Province, for those who prefer to work in French, many will be reluctant to return to the English-speaking areas of Canada.

There are still French-Canadians who console themselves by saying that, if the minorities have been able to survive since 1760, they should still be strong a century or two from now. Such an argument disregards the technological and sociological changes of the past half-century: it took two hundred years for assimilation to affect 38% of the Acadians in Nova Scotia and P.E.I. but only three decades for the next 34%; how many more years will pass before the final 28% fade away?

CHAPTER VI

The Younger Generation is Lost

Much of the euphoria surrounding the question of minority survival can be attributed to the habit of examining census figures for the population of all ages. Conclusions reached on this basis are of extremely questionable validity, due to what can only be described as a weakness in the census questionnaire.

For census purposes, "Mother Tongue" is described as being "the language first learned in childhood and still understood"; no attempt is made by the census enumerator to determine the extent to which this language is still being spoken.

Such a definition means that Mother Tongue figures are virtually valueless when studying assimilation among adult populations. All that they give is the historical record of childhood languages; they give not the slightest clue as to the languages currently favored.

However, the Mother Tongue figures for children can be usefully employed in studies of assimilation. By definition, the mother tongue given for an infant is "the language commonly spoken in the home" and, therefore, the preferred language of the child's parents.

To a fair degree of accuracy, therefore, the mother tongue figures for the 0-4 age group should, when compared with the ethnic origin figures for the same age group, give us a measure of the degree of assimilation that has occurred among the young adults, their parents. This concept was introduced in the previous chapter (Tables 11 to 13) and the measure is referred to, in this book, as the "Apparent Assimilation" for the population studied.

(It should be noted, in passing, that the error in this measure is, usually, in the direction of understating the true degree of assimilation; since we are measuring the parents through the children, accuracy would be achieved only if the assimilated families were of the same average size as those which had retained the French language.)

This chapter discusses the census figures for the younger age groups. Although these figures permit some inferences to be drawn regarding the practical difficulties to be faced if minority schools are to be established throughout Canada, the main purpose of this chapter is to present the historical trends observed among the younger generations, in the expectation that these may furnish a guide to future trends among the population as a whole.

The trend that stands out, above all others, is that each generation moves closer to complete assimilation, as the forces of the environment gradually exert their influence.

The effect of social environment and linguistically-mixed marriages is relatively slight in the more isolated rural areas and it is, of course, in just such places that the French-speaking minorities have best survived. However, the French-Canadian who moves into a city outside the Soo-Moncton limits will, immediately, be thrown into daily contact with those of the majority language; since the recent changes in the liturgy of the Catholic Church, he will, almost invariably, hear only English at even his Sunday Mass.

Very few cities can offer the French-Canadian a full social life in his own language. Generally, the parishes are mixed, with Catholics of the English language heavily predominant, so it is rare that children of French-speaking parents can be prevented from meeting and marrying fellow-parishioners of the majority language group. Even those who marry fellow French-Canadians are affected by their social as well as business contacts; they may often send their children to the English-language school even when French schools are available.

The result is that each generation moves further away from the French language. Those who were actually born in Quebec or Northern New Brunswick will, usually, retain the old tongue; their children may follow their example, but the third generation is, almost invariably, well along the road to assimilation.

Examination of the Census figures shows that the greatest migration westward from Quebec occurred during the first decade of the present century and that there has been very little movement into Western Canada during recent decades. Table 14, on the next page, shows the effects of time on the progress of assimilation, within this virtually-closed system.

In the 0-4 group, those of French mother tongue were only one-third as numerous as those of French origin. This indicates that at least two-thirds of the young adults of French origin, the parents of these children, are now English-speaking.

Table 14

Number of persons of French mother tongue vs. number of French origin, in the four Western Provinces, by age groups, 1961 Census

Age Group	*Ethnic French*	*M.T. French*	*Apparent Loss*
45-54	25,639	19,125	25%
35-44	35,227	24,533	30%
25-34	40,767	26,617	35%
15-24	45,159	24,579	46%
5-14	68,993	27,656	60%
0- 4	43,060	14,412	67%

The next table illustrates the consequences of this progressive assimilation. Outside the Soo-Moncton area, children of French mother tongue are far less numerous than seems to be generally imagined and their relative strength has declined heavily in recent decades; in several provinces, even the absolute number of French-speaking children is dropping.

Table 15

Number of children (aged 0-9) of French mother tongue, by provinces, Censuses of 1931-1961

	1931	*1941*	*1951*	*1961*
Newfoundland	n.a.	n.a.	310	371
P.E.I.	2,300	2,300	1,700	1,600
Nova Scotia	8,100	6,900	7,200	6,300
New Brunswick	39,500	41,400	56,300	59,200
Ontario	59,000	62,100	74,700	92,600
Manitoba	10,800	11,200	11,800	12,700
Saskatchewan	10,700	9,000	6,900	6,300
Alberta	6,400	6,100	6,600	7,600
British Columbia	700	900	1,600	2,200

As can be seen from the above figures, only Ontario and New Brunswick have French-speaking populations of a size sufficient to make practical a complete system of French-language schools; in both these provinces, tax support is extended to the minority schools and to the French-language universities at Ottawa and Moncton. Elsewhere, however, it is usually necessary for parents to send their children to private schools if they wish to have them truly educated in French; generally, the public school systems (and, for that matter, the parochial schools in English-predominant areas) have been an important factor in the assimilation process.

Even in Ontario and New Brunswick, however, the picture is not uniformly bright for the French-speaker. The figures of Table 15 hide the fact that, in both provinces, the French-speaking families are heavily concentrated in the counties near the Quebec border, those which lie within the Soo-Moncton limits.

Table 16

Number of children (aged 0-9), of French mother tongue and total, by regions of Ontario and New Brunswick, 1961 Census

	Population aged 0-9	*M.T. French*
New Brunswick:		
7 northern counties	92,553	57,160
8 southern counties	61,889	1,998
Ontario:		
11 border counties	268,900	76,700
Elsewhere	1,145,800	15,889

Examination of the above table shows that the French-speaking children of the southern areas of both provinces are so small a part of the total school-aged population (just over 1% in Ontario, 3% in New Brunswick) that their existence actually hampers the progress of their co-linguists living in the border counties. Many of the legislators at Toronto and Fredericton represent ridings in which the speaking of French is regarded as merely a gesture of defiance; it is difficult for them to realize, and to convince their voters, that some parts of their provinces actually do contain French-speaking populations sizable enough to justify the existence of a school system in that language.

Looking at the entire area of Canada outside the Soo-Moncton limits, we find that there were, in 1961, only 55,000 children of French-speaking families dispersed among two-and-a-half million English-speaking children. Even if separate classes were to be provided for all the French-speaking children, the daily contact in the playgrounds and on the streets (where

English is, almost invariably, the only language heard) would suffice to lead most young French-Canadians well along the path to assimilation.

The status of the minority group is quite different within the Province of Quebec, where the English-speaking children have actually increased in relative strength during recent decades; although partly attributable to postwar immigration, the major cause of the recovery has been the larger family size now prevalent among English-speaking Canadians.

Table 17

Number of Children (aged 0-9) of English, of French and of Other Mother Tongues, Quebec Province, Censuses of 1931-1961

	1931	*1941*	*1951*	*1961*
M.T. French	606,100	615,600	874,800	1,092,700
M.T. English	74,100	66,600	112,800	155,300
Other M.T.'s	26,500	19,100	17,300	47,300

Despite a drop during the Depression years, the English-speaking population of school age has more than doubled since 1931, while children from French-speaking families were increasing by only 80%. In 1931, the 138,000 French-speaking children living in the other provinces were far more numerous than Quebec's minority groups; today, the 189,000 French-speaking children in the nine provinces are probably outnumbered by the English-speaking children of Quebec (after taking into account those of other mother tongues who are now being brought up in English).

Although 70% of the English-speaking children are to be found within the limits of Metropolitan Montreal, the 50,000 dispersed throughout the rest of the province are almost equal in numbers to the entire French-speaking school-aged population of New Brunswick and are eight times as numerous as the French-speaking children of such provinces as Nova Scotia and Saskatchewan. Taking into account the financial resources available to the English-speaking population, it can be appreciated that the minority in Quebec has never had difficulty in providing satisfactory educational facilities for those who wished to study in English.

It has, in fact, been a source of no little irritation to French-Canadians that the English-language educational system in Quebec has been, for many years, vastly superior to that provided for the majority of the young French-speaking citizens of the one province in Canada in which the

French language might expect preference. Reliance on local realty taxes for the support of each school board, the root of this problem, meant that the money available for the education of the average English-speaking pupil was many times that which could be raised per French-speaking child.

Recent changes in the philosophy of school-tax collection have greatly helped the French-language schools of Ontario and Quebec as equalization funds drawn from the general revenues of the provinces supplement the local taxes in the poorer areas; similar assistance is soon to be introduced in New Brunswick. This, and the various social security measures put into effect by the federal and provincial governments in recent years, should have the effect of considerably upgrading the average level of education among the French-speaking population living within the Soo-Moncton limits.

For the minorities elsewhere, however, and this applies also to the English-speaking minority in the more remote parts of Quebec Province, recent developments in education have increased the problems involved in survival. When the Separate Schools Act came into force in Ontario in 1855, it permitted a school to be established whenever 15 children of a minority could be found within a radius of three miles. In 1964, however, the then Minister of Education of Quebec informed the Anglo-Protestants of Pontiac County that no school region could be set up to serve less than 1,000 pupils and that their children would, under a reorganization of the school system then in progress, have to go all the way to Hull (75 miles distant) if they wished to complete their secondary education in their own language.

In every province of Canada, the schools are being consolidated into larger units which must draw their pupils from ever-widening districts. In the rural areas, particularly, this has played an important part in breaking down the old isolation; no longer is it possible to maintain schools in which only French (or, on the Prairies, only Ukrainian!) will be heard. In these larger schools, children from the French and other minority groups will be thrown into contact with other children who speak only English and the latter language will, almost invariably, be acquired on the play-ground as well as in the classrooms.

The segregation that was possible in the days of small schools drawing from homogeneous localities is indicated by the figures of the following table. In the rural areas of New Brunswick, it is very striking that less than half the French-speaking population of post-school age claimed to be bilingual; even in Ontario, many rural French-Canadians did not learn English until well on in their teens.

Table 18

Percentages of Population of French Mother Tongue speaking "French Only", by Age Groups, for Rural and Urban Areas, Ontario and New Brunswick, 1961 Census

	5-9	*10-14*	*15-19*
New Brunswick:			
Rural Farm	95%	84%	56%
Rural non-farm	88	76	51
Urban	55	35	18
Ontario:			
Rural Farm	66	43	22
Rural non-farm	49	26	14
Urban	29	11	6

With the exception of a few small pockets, such as that around St. Boniface, where the French-Canadian population has been large enough to permit a continuation of French-language instruction in the schools and, even more important, to minimize social intermingling and the incidence of linguistically-mixed marriages, the younger generation outside the Soo-Moncton limits has been largely lost to the French language. Increasing urbanization and the greater mobility of adolescents may well destroy even the present few pockets of resistance within another generation.

There are, of course, persons of both language groups who claim, in all sincerity, that the provision of French-language schools and television from coast to coast would permit survival of the present French-speaking minorities. This seems to disregard the social and economic factors leading to assimilation.

Quebec is the only province in which full economic opportunity is available to those who prefer to work in French. Only in Quebec, or in the border regions of Ontario and New Brunswick, will a full cultural and social life be available in French and only within these restricted limits will the young French-Canadian be certain of finding a wife of his own language group.

If the children are not educated in French, then the minorities will dwindle away through assimilation; if French schools are provided, then the probability exists that their graduates will migrate to Quebec when the time comes to leave home and seek employment. In either case, the end result is the same: no younger generation will remain to replace the ageing group who now speak French outside the Soo-Moncton limits.

CHAPTER VII

No Reinforcements from Quebec

If the younger generation is almost totally lost to the French language, as concluded in the previous chapter, can the French-speaking minorities outside the Soo-Moncton limits be kept alive through migration from the over-populated rural areas of Quebec and Northern New Brunswick?

Historically, of course, the French language was carried throughout Central and Western Canada by migrants from the old parishes along the St. Lawrence. However, the movement westward was never as heavy as that toward the United States and, at least as far as the Prairie Provinces are concerned, seems to have stopped almost completely some thirty-five years ago.

The 1941 Census found that, of the 138,000 persons of French mother tongue living in the four Western Provinces, only 26,000 had been born in Eastern Canada (21,300 in Quebec, 3,500 in Ontario and 700 in New Brunswick); this was hardly more than the 16,400 who had been born outside Canada.

Since that time, there appears to have been very little net movement of French-Canadians or Acadians into the West, the surplus population of the rural counties of French Canada preferring to seek their fortunes in the industrial centres of Quebec or Ontario or the United States.

There are, unfortunately, no figures available for the interprovincial migration of French-Canadians since 1941, the Dominion Bureau of Statistics no longer making any breakdown of migrants by language groups. The figures of the following table, however, would appear to indicate that there has been very little net flow of French-speaking Canadians into the West during the past twenty years (some 2,000 French-speaking male immigrants arrived from abroad during this postwar period).

Table 19

Number of Male persons of French Mother Tongue, by specified Groups of Birth Dates, Western Provinces, Censuses of 1941 and of 1961

Years of Birth	*1941*	*1961*	*Change*
1907-1916	10,700	9,760	—9%
1917-1926	13,385	12,405	—7%
1927-1936	13,792	13,767	—
1937-1941	6,811	6,396	—6%

Turning to Ontario, we find that migration, in both directions, has been relatively heavy across the border with Quebec: the Census reported 8,000 persons annually moving from Ontario into Quebec while 11,000 were moving from Quebec into Ontario and an additional 2,500 from New Brunswick into Ontario (during the period 1956-1961).

Any attempt to analyze these figures runs up against the insurmountable problem that no breakdown is available by language groups. Many of those moving from Ontario into Quebec would be French-Canadians returning to their original homeland (including about 1,000 annually who move from Ottawa into the suburbs on the Quebec side of the river) but a considerable number would be English-speaking professional and technical men (and their families) moving to new jobs in Montreal or elsewhere. The problem is even greater when it comes to treating the movement into Ontario from New Brunswick and Quebec, since much of the latter would be of postwar immigrants moving further inland after a brief stay at Montreal.

We can say, with complete certainty, that not all the 13,500 moving annually to Ontario would be French-speaking; we may guess that the proportion would be rather less than half. As against this movement of probably well under 35,000 Acadians and French-Canadians into Ontario, that province received over 340,000 immigrants from abroad during the period 1956-1961 and well over three-quarters of a million babies were born to Ontario families during the same five years.

In other words, the number of French-speaking migrants entering Ontario, although substantial when compared to the few going to the West, represents, at the very most, less than 3% of the increase in population from other sources and is not nearly of a magnitude that will change the linguistic complexion of the province.

On the contrary, as the figures of the following table indicate, the inflow of French-speakers, in recent decades, has little more than balanced the departure of those returning to Quebec or emigrating to the United States; due allowance made for the 3,000 foreign-born males of French mother tongue who came to Ontario between 1941 and 1961, it is apparent that the net reinforcement received by the Franco-Ontarians from Quebec and New Brunswick has been virtually negligible.

Table 20

Number of Male Persons of French Mother Tongue, by specified Groups of Birth Dates, Ontario, Censuses of 1941-1961

	Census of		
Years of Birth	*1941*	*1951*	*1961*
1907-1916	23,800	23,700	21,900
1917-1926	28,800	29,600	29,600
1927-1936	30,900	32,000	34,700
1937-1946	—	33,300	34,800

The reduced rate of migration toward Ontario and the Western Provinces in recent decades reflects, at least in part, the disillusionment of the French-Canadian with the old doctrine that his destiny was to work the soil. No longer are the marginal farm lands of Northern Ontario (or even the good soil of the Peace River Country) capable of attracting farmers' sons from the over-populated rural parishes of Quebec; it is, rather, to the cities that the new generation are heading.

The industrial development of Quebec has, therefore, played an important role in the reduction of movement toward the other provinces. If sufficient new jobs can be created at Montreal or Sept-Iles or Sainte-Thérèse, there will be no need for the French-Canadian worker to migrate into areas where he must learn a new language if he wishes to have any hope for advancement.

However, the number of new jobs needed is considerable, and will continue to be high for many years, despite the recent drop in birth rates among French-Canadians, as the children of the past two decades reach the age at which they must seek employment.

Some indication of the magnitude of this problem can be obtained by studying the figures of the next table. During the decade 1951-1961, some 240,000 persons (chiefly French-speaking, although no breakdown is given by the Census) left the rural areas of Quebec and Northern New Brunswick, presumably to seek work at Montreal or in other industrial areas.

When projecting this figure into the future, it should be remembered that there were only 787,000 children born in Quebec between 1931 and 1940 (those reaching their majority during the 1951-61 period); 1,343,000 births were recorded during the 1951-1961 decade.

Table 21

Immigration, Natural Increase and apparent net Domestic Migration, by sub-regions, Quebec Province and Northern New Brunswick, 1951-1961

	Immigrants Arriving	*Natural Increase*	*Internal Movement**
Areas of net outward movement:			
Northern New Brunswick	2,400	79,500	—41,900
Gaspe & Lower St. Lawrence	700	106,500	—66,300
Lake St. John	1,000	73,600	—10,100
Abitibi-Temiscamingue	2,400	49,400	—24,700
Eastern Townships	3,800	55,300	—14,200
Elsewhere in Quebec	9,000	269,300	—83,300
Sub-total	19,300	633,600	—240,500
Areas of net inward movement:			
Montreal	185,300	349,800	+150,900
Quebec	3,800	54,700	+19,900
Hull	1,000	18,900	+7,500
Lower North Shore	2,300	20,800	+16,200
Sub-total	192,400	444,200	+194,500
Total:	211,700	1,077,800	—46,000

*Net movement: a (—) sign indicates that this net movement was outward; a (+) sign shows that the area attracted newcomers from other parts of Canada, in excess of those leaving.

The second part of the above table shows that Montreal was able to absorb over 150,000 newcomers from other parts of Canada, in addition to 185,000 immigrants from abroad and almost 350,000 of its own natural increase. However, other areas of the province showed very little absorptive capacity — Quebec City took hardly more than did the iron ore country of the Lower North Shore — and there was a net outward migration of some 46,000 persons from Quebec Province and Northern New Brunswick.

(Note that this was a NET outward movement; as perhaps 80,000 persons moved into Quebec from Ontario during the decade, the actual outward migration would have taken some 125,000 persons into Ontario and the United States or elsewhere.)

The policy of the present Quebec Government, as of its predecessor, is to create jobs within the province. By the attraction of private capital or through the establishment of state enterprises, industry is to be expanded. At the same time, great emphasis is being placed on the education of adults, as well as of children, so that French-Canadians may, to an increasing extent, fill positions at all levels.

The Quiet Revolution began only in the Fall of 1959 and there has not yet been time for its effects to become fully felt. However, if all hopes are fulfilled and if there is a satisfactory level of opportunity available within Quebec in future years, then there will be very little incentive for French-Canadians to seek work elsewhere; this will be particularly true if the language of work in Quebec factories becomes French, since men trained only in that language will be less easily able to move to an equivalent job in an English-speaking city.

As the universities and trade schools of Quebec begin to meet the needs of their province's commerce and industry, there may well be a reduction in the inward flow of English-speaking technicians and professional men from other provinces. It is even possible that net migration of English-speakers will become heavily outward, as those who prefer to work in their own language leave Quebec to seek employment elsewhere.

Historically, the cross-migration of the two language groups has been motivated by economic factors. Although the seminaries of Quebec prepared many priests and religious for work in other parts of Canada, the typical French-Canadian leaving his home province did so to find work in occupations at the low end of the wage scale: in the early years, he went west to paddle the canoe of a Scottish fur-trader and in more recent years he has been recruited for the logging camps of Northern Ontario or for the mills of New Westminster and Welland.

In contrast, many English-speaking persons came to Quebec during the 19th Century as members of the Civil or Military Establishment; others, particularly from New England and Scotland, were entrepreneurs setting up sawmills or commercial establishments. In recent decades, engineers and other professionals have been brought in from universities all over Canada, to staff the plants at Shawinigan and Arvida and Schefferville and the head offices and laboratories at Montreal.

These patterns are changing. It is, already, uneconomical for industries in other provinces to recruit French-Canadian labor forces; when Quebec can provide its own professionals, then each language group will tend to be employed only on its own side of the linguistic frontier, driving the final nail into the coffin of the minorities.

CHAPTER VIII

La Revanche des Berceaux

Although the expression itself is quite familiar to most English-speaking Canadians, the full significance that "La Revanche des Berceaux" has had for French-Canadians can only be grasped by reading eulogies such as the following, in which the local French-language newspaper praises the virtues of a man from Beauce County who left some 600 descendants when he finally died at the age of 96:

> "The grandfather of Mr. Philippon met an honorable death at the Battle of the Plains of Abraham; his grandson has well revenged this death by adding, through his own (sic!) efforts, an entire parish to French Canada."

Even during the insurrections of 1837, the French-Canadians had little expectation of reconquering the colony through force of arms. Until quite recently, however, they did, most earnestly, hope that the high rate of natural increase of the French-speaking population would, eventually, bring it to political dominance.

To encourage this hope, they could point to the historical fact that, during the last half of the Nineteenth Century and the early decades of the present century, an outpouring of surplus population from the rural parishes had succeeded in reversing the language picture at Montreal and in almost submerging the English language in such regions as the Eastern Townships and the Ottawa Valley.

The severe decline in birth rates among Canadians of British origin after World War I and the virtual cessation of immigration after 1930 were both factors encouraging this French dream. By the late 1930's, demographers of both language groups were beginning to admit the possibility of a Canada in which those of French mother tongue would be in the majority.

Even today, the illusion is not quite dissipated that rural Quebec is an inexhaustible source of new French-Canadians and that time is on the side of the French language. The cold statistics, however, show that the reverse is now true.

Contrary to popular belief, the birth rate among French-Canadians has never been really phenomenal. At its peak, it was no higher than that prevailing generally among all ethnic groups in North America a century or so ago; the only exceptional factor was that families of French origin were slower than others to adopt limitations on the number of children.

At present, the typical family size among French-Canadians living in Montreal is hardly different from that observed among persons of British origin living in Toronto. However, one-third of the French-Canadians are still living in rural areas where families (among those of all origins) are usually more numerous than in the cities; in these areas, too, the old propaganda of the French-Canadian "nationalists" still lingers and there is more social pressure toward large families than would be found elsewhere.

The following table gives a ratio obtained by dividing the number of women of child-bearing age into the number of children aged 0-14. Unlike some other indices, this takes into account the effects of the most prevalent family-control measure practised in French Canada, the postponement of marriage (in 1961, 32% of the French-origin women in Quebec aged 15 years or over were still single, as compared to only 20% for British-origin women of the same age in Ontario). The actual figures have no significance in themselves but they do permit a comparison to be made between different ethnic groups and census years.

Table 22

Ratio of Children (0-14) to Women (20-44) among Population of British Origin in Ontario vs. that among Population of French Origin in Quebec, by Rural and Urban, Censuses of 1931-1961

	1931	*1941*	*1951*	*1961*
Of British origin, Ontario —				
rural	1.82	1.59	1.97	2.45
urban	1.23	1.05	1.22	1.74
all	1.42	1.22	1.39	1.88
Of French origin, Quebec —				
rural	3.00	2.66	2.86	3.20
urban	1.81	1.45	1.53	1.90
all	2.22	1.85	1.92	2.20

In 1931 and 1941, there were, for each French-origin woman living in Quebec, 50% more children than for her British-origin counterpart living in Ontario. By 1951, the difference had begun to narrow and the latest Census showed a gap of only 17%, a gap which may well disappear as the population of Quebec becomes increasingly urban.

However, comparison of French Quebec with British Ontario gives only part of the story, since the latter province is heavily urbanized and has a lower birth rate than that found in many other parts of English-speaking Canada. In Newfoundland, for example, the population of British origin had a child/woman ratio of 3.03 in 1961, only slightly below that of even the rural French-Canadians. For Canada as a whole, the ratio for those of British origin was 2.01 as against 2.25 for those of French origin and "La Revanche" has now become only a discredited dream.

If we consider all those of English mother tongue (rather than merely those of British origin), then the heavy upturn in the non-French birth rate in recent years is reflected in the figures of the following table.

Table 23

Number of Children of English, of French and of Other Mother Tongues, Canada, Censuses of 1931-1961

	1931	*1941*	*1951*	*1961*
French	33.7%	36.0%	33.4%	29.6%
English	51.4	51.4	60.1	62.6
Others	14.9	12.6	6.5	7.8
	100.0%	100.0%	100.0%	100.0%

In 1931, the proportion of French-Canadians among the children had been well above that for the adult population (24.0%) but the spread actually widened even further during the next ten years and, by 1941, the propagandists of La Revanche were preparing a victory celebration. This proved premature, as can be seen from the last two columns of the above table, and by 1961 the proportion of children who reported their mother tongue as French was only slightly higher than the 26.4% which their language group represented among the adult population.

The three factors which combined to wipe out the French gains of 1931-1941 were:

1. A substantial increase in the birth rate of those of other origins during recent years.

2. Resumption of immigration on a large scale in the postwar years, with the children of immigrants generally assimilating to the English-speaking community.

3. Assimilation, on an increasing scale, of the younger generation of French ethnics living outside the Soo-Moncton limits (if the above table had been on the basis of ethnic origins, rather than of mother tongues, the French figure would have been 33.4% in 1961 vs. 34.8% in 1931).

Weighing the relative values of these three factors, we can say that, among the children reporting their mother tongue as English in 1961, approximately 6% did so as a consequence of the assimilation of French-speaking ancestors and a further 29% would have been of origins other than British or French. This leaves 65% as the contribution of British-origin families and shows the important role played by the postwar rise in the average size of such families.

Turning now to the most recent trends, we must switch our base and examine current vital statistics by provinces, as there is no breakdown available by language groups. Although this introduces some inaccuracies, it does, at least, permit the drawing of some important inferences.

Despite recent declines observed everywhere in North America, the latest figures show that there had been 19.1 births for every 1,000 persons living in Canada outside Quebec, during the 12-month period ended September 30, 1967.

Inside Quebec, however, the birth rate for the same period was only 17.9, which represented an almost unbelievable drop from the 28.5 reported as recently as 1959 and from the 31.1 peak reached in 1947. After deducting deaths, Quebec's natural increase in population during the period was only 66,000, as compared to an average of over 104,000 during the years 1956-1960.

The entire pattern of family life in French Canada has changed during the past quarter century. Even outside the cities, television has introduced new concepts and new scales of values; no longer is the size of the family dictated by old rural ideals, and the younger generation of French-Canadians is increasingly eager to have a greater share of worldly goods.

There are, even today, a few "last-ditch" nationalists who still hope that present trends can be reversed and who have been asking the provincial legislature to institute payment of family allowances on an ascending scale, as is now done in France, to encourage an increase in family size.

The more realistic demographers, however, point out that urbanization is increasing, with over half the population of Quebec already living in the three metropolitan centres (Montreal, Quebec and Hull) and that this, in combination with greater emancipation of Quebec women and the rise in general educational levels, can only result in a further downward movement of the province's birth rate.

"La Revanche des Berceaux", therefore, has now passed into the realm of fantasy.

CHAPTER IX

Immigration — 95% English-speaking

If, as outlined in the previous chapter, the trend in birth rates is such that the rates of natural increase of the two language groups will soon be almost identical, then there will be only two factors left to cause their relative strengths to change: assimilation and net migration. The first of these factors has been discussed in a previous chapter.

Immigration into Canada is currently running at somewhat over 150,000 persons annually. Of these, however, a few return to their former countries and many continue on into the United States; the number actually taking up permanent residence in Canada would be in the vicinity of 100,000 annually.

The importance of an immigration which adds a million persons to the population of Canada during each decade can best be appreciated by comparison with the number of children born in Canada during the same period.

The 1961 Census found 4,336,000 children aged 0-9 in Canada, of whom 131,000 had been foreign-born. Among the Canadian-born children, just over 30% had been of French mother tongue but immigration helped drop the relative strength of the French-Canadians from 29.0% in 1951 to 28.1% in 1961.

It is evident, from the following figures, that the foreign-born population of Canada has shown an overwhelming preference for English over French; excluding those who had not learned either of the two "official" languages, 98% could speak English as against only 10% who could speak French, although less than half these immigrants had been of English mother tongue.

Table 24

Number of Persons speaking English and speaking French among Foreign-born residents of Canada, by Years of Entry into Canada, 1961 Census

Date of Entry into Canada	*English Only**	*English & French**	*French Only**	*Neither Language*
pre-1921	700,000	50,000	10,000	12,000
1921-1930	411,000	26,000	3,000	5,000
1931-1945	103,000	14,000	2,000	2,000
Total pre-war	1,214,000	90,000	15,000	19,000
	91%	7%	1%	1%
Post-war	1,229,000	126,000	47,000	106,000
	82%	8%	3%	7%

*In addition to any languages other than English & French.

Table 25 is, perhaps, even more significant than the previous, since it shows that immigrants living in the only province in Canada with a French-speaking majority have, by a substantial margin, favored the English language. This is particularly remarkable when it is considered that those who entered after the war included only 54,000 of English mother tongue, as compared to 31,500 French and 59,000 Italians.

Table 25

Number of Persons speaking English and speaking French among Foreign-born residents ot Quebec, by Years of Entry into Canada, 1961 Census

Entered Canada	*English Only*	*English & French*	*French Only*	*Neither Language*
Before 1946	77,000	49,000	13,000	2,000
	55%	35%	9%	1%
1946-1961	115,000	61,000	43,000	29,000
	46%	25%	17%	12%

Another way of establishing the preference for English among immigrants is to examine the census figures for the mother tongues of those of various ethnic origins. This method has several weaknesses, one being that the Census does not differentiate between, for example, the children of recent arrivals and those whose families have been in Canada for two centuries (e.g., descendants of the 18th Century founders of Lunenburg), but it does give us a relative scale. The following table is for four representative metropolitan areas; other cities would follow the pattern noted in Toronto, with negligible assimilation toward the French language.

Table 26

Percentage giving English as Mother Tongue, among Persons of Specified Ethnic Groups giving English or French as Mother Tongue, specified Metropolitan Areas, 1961 Census

	Quebec	*Montreal*	*Ottawa/Hull*	*Toronto*
All ethnics except British & French	26%	76%	90%	99%
Including:				
Italian	15	32	87	99
German	29	77	94	99
Polish	31	83	95	99
Ukrainian	42	81	96	99

The preceding table indicates that very few immigrants are bringing up their children in the French language. This is true even in Montreal, where almost all ethnic groups, with the notable exception of the Italians, show a better than three-to-one preference for English.

Several factors have contributed to this preference. The foremost, probably, is that most immigrants have come, not just to Quebec Province, but to North America. To have freedom of movement on this continent, to ensure that their children will be able to speak to their cousins in Toronto or New York, English is essential. French, on the other hand, can be used in only one corner of the continent and, even there, is not absolutely necessary.

Other reasons stem from the essentially closed nature of French Canada. The Protestant immigrant from Switzerland or the Jew from North Africa has, until very recently, been forced to send his children to English-language schools, only Catholics being admitted to most of the

French-language schools of Quebec. Thus, French Canada has forced into the other language group many of those immigrants who spoke French before coming to Canada and has attracted to itself only those few immigrants who were susceptible to intermarriage (chiefly Italians in recent years, Irish in the 19th Century).

Tables 24 to 26 have given a clear indication that immigrants show a preference for the English language. In an attempt to quantify this preference, let us follow one particular group, those born during the five years 1927 to 1931.

The 1941 Census reported 1,100,871 persons aged 10-14 living in Canada. Twenty years later, the 1961 Census found 1,271,810 persons aged 30-34. Allowing for mortality and for possible errors in enumeration, we can conclude that net immigration contributed somewhat over 200,000 persons to this group.

Of these additions to Canada's population, just over half were of English mother tongue while, as the following table shows, immigration of persons of French mother tongue did not even balance the losses due to mortality and emigration.

Table 27

Number of Persons of English, of French and of Other Mother Tongues, born 1927-1931, enumerated in Canada at Census of 1941 vs. Census of 1961

Mother Tongue	*1941 Census*	*1961 Census*	*Change*
French	381,004	356,705	—24,299
English	568,622	672,170	+103,548
Others	151,245	242,935	+91,690

Thanks to immigration, those of English mother tongue slightly increased their relative strength among the population of this age group while those of French mother tongue dropped from 34.6% in 1941 to 28.1% in 1961.

However, this is not the complete story, since it does not indicate the preference for English among immigrants of mother tongues other than the two discussed. For a measure of this preference, let us look at some further figures for the same age group.

Table 28

Number of Persons claiming ability to speak English and to speak French, born 1927-1931, enumerated in Canada at Census of 1941 vs. Census of 1961

Languages Spoken	*1941 Census*	*1961 Census*	*Change*
French Only	305,768	188,430	—117,338
French & English	96,206	229,133	+132,927
English Only	694,933	839,262	+144,329
Neither	3,970	14,985	+11,015

Adding the "French Only" to the "French & English", we find that those capable of speaking French totalled 418,000 in 1961, as against 402,000 in 1941. Deducting the numbers of those for whom French was the mother tongue, we find that those claiming ability to speak French as a second or third language had risen from 21,000 in 1941 to 61,000 in 1961.

As the latter figure represented only 7% of the non-French population of this age group, the twenty-year increase was hardly more than might have been expected from the learning of French by Canadians of other languages who had still been attending school in 1941. These figures would appear to confirm the conclusion drawn from Table 24, that the vast majority of 1941-1961 immigrants have not felt that a knowledge of French is necessary.

The age group selected for our study is the one which has been in the family-forming stage during the past decade and which is now bringing up the citizens of tomorrow. Thus, there is a multiplying factor which must be considered: for each immigrant who assimilates to the English-speaking population, there will be Canadian-born children brought up with a preference for the English language.

The French-Canadian studying the demographic history of our country never fails to remark on the importance of immigration in maintaining the minority position of his own group. Each time that the French-speaking population began to gain ground through their higher birth rate, a fresh wave of immigrants (not necessarily of English mother tongue, but assimilating to the English-speaking group) would arrive to wipe out the temporary gain.

Table 29, on the following page, shows the numerical importance of immigrants. However, these immigrants added more than mere numbers to English Canada; the knowledge and skills they brought with them further widened the disparity in average educational levels between Canada's two major language groups.

Table 29

Foreign-born Population vs. Total Population of Canada, Censuses of 1871-1961

	1871	*1901*	*1931*	*1961*
Total population	3,486	5,371	10,377	18,238
Foreign-born	585	700	2,281	2,844
Foreign-born/Total	17%	13%	22%	16%

The effects of immigration are, of course, not felt equally by all parts of the country. In the four Atlantic Provinces, there are only 67,000 foreign-born among a total population of almost two million, so their influence is minimal. At the other extreme, the 607,000 immigrants living at Toronto make up one-third of the total population of that metropolitan area; as the majority of these arrived after the end of the War, they have completely changed the aspect of the city during the past two decades.

A breakdown of immigrant population by provinces shows that over half of those who arrived after 1945 are now living in Ontario, 405,000 of them at Toronto. Montreal attracted some 214,000 postwar immigrants but only 34,000 settled in other parts of Quebec Province. The Western Provinces, Saskatchewan in particular, have never regained their pre-1930 popularity and the Atlantic Provinces have long been an area of net emigration.

Table 30

Foreign-born Population by Province of Residence and by Date of Entry into Canada, 1961 Census

	Date of Immigration	
	pre-1946	*1946-1961*
Atlantic Provinces	34,000	32,000
Quebec	141,000	248,000
Ontario	520,000	833,000
Manitoba	108,000	62,000
Saskatchewan	120,000	29,000
Alberta	167,000	122,000
British Columbia	246,000	177,000
Canada	1,337,000	1,507,000

It might be noted in passing that 76% of the pre-war and 87% of post-war immigrants live in urban areas. Only 10% of the pre-war and 5% of the post-war immigrants were found on farms and the remainder are in rural areas but not on farms.

Almost one-quarter of the adults living in Canada in 1961 had been born outside the country. Their coming has added not only numbers but, also, valuable skills to the strength of the English-speaking population to which nearly all of them have assimilated. Conversely, the failure of the French-speaking community to attract to itself any significant number of immigrants has weakened it both quantitatively and qualitatively.

CHAPTER X

The Minority Newspapers — A Barometer?

Perhaps it is due to the fact that a coin must be paid over, but the average person exercises a deliberate act of choice each time that he picks up a newspaper, quite unlike the random manner in which the dial of a television set may be turned.

The circulation of the minority newspapers should, therefore, be a barometer of the strength of their language group in any area. When we see, for example, that the circulation of the Sherbrooke Record is barely holding the level reached fifteen years ago, while that of La Tribune de Sherbrooke has doubled during the same period, we may infer that the English language is losing ground in the Eastern Townships. Conversely, the fact that L'Evangeline has a circulation of only 10,000, while the English-language newspapers of New Brunswick sell 90,000 copies daily, would lead us to examine with considerable scepticism any claim that the French language is approaching the importance of English in that province.

Outside the Province of Quebec, there are only two daily newspapers published in French. These are located in the major urban centres of the Acadians and the Franco-Ontarians, respectively, and each serves its own group. The last French-language daily in the United States ceased publication in 1962.

L'Evangeline was founded in 1887, as a weekly newspaper published in Weymouth, an Acadian town in the southwestern tip of Nova Scotia. Publication was moved to Moncton a few years later, but it was not until 1930 that the Acadian resurgence had become strong enough to justify a daily newspaper; due to the Depression, this lasted for only 13 months.

In 1942, a new archbishop was appointed to Moncton and began an aggressive campaign in favor of the French language. As part of this campaign, contributions were solicited in Quebec and the Maritimes to permit increasing the frequency of publication of L'Evangeline; by September, 1949, this was again a daily newspaper.

At present, the audited circulation is in the vicinity of 10,000, at which level the paper cannot break even, financially. However, campaigns which are given the active support of Quebec French-language newspapers and "patriotic" societies supply the funds required to keep the paper alive; in recent years, these voluntary contributions have been supplemented by grants, totalling over $112,000, from the Cultural Affairs Department of the Government of Quebec.

The greatest problem to be overcome by L'Evangeline appears to be the indifference of the Acadian masses. The potential readership is at least 260,000 (210,000 in New Brunswick, the others in Nova Scotia and P.E.I.), which means that only one Acadian in 26 is buying the paper; with a potential readership of just under 400,000, the five English-language daily newspapers published in New Brunswick have a total circulation of some 90,000.

It is difficult to forecast the future of L'Evangeline. Publishing costs have been rising, all over the continent, and there is a limit to what can be accomplished by goodwill and devotion alone. However, the paper's management and finances were completely reorganized at the end of 1966 and continued existence, on a subsidized basis, appears to have been assured through association with La Société l'Assomption, the Acadians' fraternal insurance company which operates in New England as well as in the Maritimes and which has assets of about $30 million.

Turning from the anaemic financial condition of the Acadians' paper, it may surprise some readers to learn that the Franco-Ontarians' publishing company reported a net profit of over $30,000 for the year ended December 31, 1966; gross revenue included $2,225,000 from the newspaper itself and $1,746,000 from the commercial printing division.

Le Droit has three important advantages over L'Evangeline:

1) The French-speaking population of Ontario is double that of New Brunswick.

2) Its border location permits Le Droit to include, among its potential readers, the 150,000 French-speaking residents of Western Quebec.

3) The revenues of the newspaper are heavily supplemented by those from a large job-printing plant; this does not rely merely on its captive market (the archdiocese), but aggressively solicits outside business, in both languages.

Although financially successful, Le Droit has experienced several notable setbacks in its efforts to be not only a local newspaper for the residents of Hull/Ottawa but, also, a militant organ for French-speaking minorities elsewhere. In June, 1963, the Northern Edition had to be discontinued; despite 15 years of promotional effort and the support of the bishops of Northern Ontario, circulation had never reached the break-even point (it is, perhaps, not entirely coincidental that this is an area in which assimilation is beginning to make heavy inroads among the younger generation).

In 1965, total paid circulation of Le Droit was just under 35,000 copies daily; this was less than half the circulation of each of the two English-language dailies published in Ottawa but appears quite adequate to ensure that the Franco-Ontarians will continue to have their newspaper for many years to come.

Le Droit's position, as the semi-official voice of the most important French-speaking group outside Quebec, makes it doubly unfortunate that the editorial policy of this paper still retains the anglophobic spirit in which it was born, during the most bitter days of the 1913 school dispute (when the French language was banned from the tax-supported schools of Ontario). Interestingly enough, for a paper so closely linked with a religious order, the English-speaking bishops of Southern Ontario are not exempt from attack and are often blamed for the high rate of assimilation that has occurred in their dioceses.

Turning now to another minority, only 700,000 residents of Quebec Province gave English as their mother tongue, in 1961; this was hardly more than the 690,000 French-speaking residents of Ontario and the Maritimes, but the four English-language dailies published in Quebec have a total circulation of almost 350,000. There is, consequently, no doubt as to the continuing existence of the Montreal Gazette (135,000 circulation) or the Montreal Star (195,000), although some reservations may be held as to the length of life left for the Quebec Chronicle-Telegraph (5,400) and the Sherbrooke Record (8,900), both of which serve areas in which the relative importance of the English language has declined heavily in recent decades.

Quebec, Ontario and New Brunswick being the only provinces in which large linguistic minorities are to be found, they are, also, the only provinces in which daily newspapers are published in the respective minority languages. The French-speaking minorities living outside the Soo-Moncton limits are served only by weeklies, of which the circulation is seldom more than 2,000-3,000 copies.

The most important French-language paper in the West is "La Liberté et le Patriote", published at St. Boniface as the consolidation of two newspapers founded at the same time as Le Droit; its circulation of some 8,000 copies is several times the average for papers of this nature and reflects the strength of the French-speaking population in this particular area.

Further west, it is an interesting commentary on the ethno-linguistic makeup of the population of the Prairies that "La Survivance" of Edmonton has fewer than 2,500 subscribers while the "Ukrainian News", published in the same city, can sell 9,000 copies weekly.

At the other end of the country, the Diocese of Yarmouth is served by "Le Petit Courrier"; founded in 1937, this has a circulation of just under 2,000. Nova Scotia would, however, be within the fringes of the area served by L'Evangeline, so the weeklies are not quite as important here as they would be in the Western Provinces.

The Census of Canada is taken only every ten years and there can be considerable change within such a period. If used with discretion, the circulation figures for the minority newspapers may furnish a useful interim guide as to the progress of their language group in any specified area.

CHAPTER XI

The Fatal Hemorrhage

From the very founding of the colony along the St. Lawrence, the promise of a better material life has served to draw French-Canadians southward. In 1682, William Penn published a circular inviting Canadians to move down to Pennsylvania; during the 19th Century his example was followed by the entrepreneurs of New England, who sought dependable but inexpensive labor for their new mills.

Although the great exodus of French-Canadians toward the United States was one of the decisive factors contributing to the supremacy of the English language in Canada, the importance and extent of this movement are seldom fully appreciated. The figures, however, are to be found in the Census of the United States and in the immigration reports of that country.

The 1900 Census classed 851,000 residents of the United States as being of French-Canadian origin (a figure which included only immigrants and the children of immigrants; subsequent generations are not identified). As the total number of persons shown by the 1901 Census of Canada as being of French origin was only 1,649,000, it is clear that the southward migration of the 19th Century had affected well over one-third of the descendants of the original French colonists.

At the beginning of this century, the west of Canada was still relatively empty. Within what are now the three Prairie Provinces, the 1901 Census found only 415,000 persons, of whom 23,000 were of French origin.

What would have happened if even half of the southward migration of Quebec's surplus population had been diverted into the Canadian West, as Archbishop Taché and others tried so hard to effect? To what language would the newcomers from Eastern Europe have assimilated if they had come into provinces with French-speaking majorities and French-language school systems? Would we now have a French-speaking country extending from the Bay of Fundy to the Peace River, surrounded by a United States that would include British Columbia, Southern Ontario and the Atlantic Provinces?

This is a fascinating topic for speculation, but the fact remains that the French-Canadians did NOT go west in any numbers, preferring work at steady wages in New England and mill towns to the hardships of homesteading on the Prairies. The decisions made by these hundreds of thousands of individuals doomed the French language in Western Canada.

Migration across the border was chiefly northward during the first three-quarters of a century after 1760. By 1833, the southward flow had barely reached one thousand persons annually and the real flood did not develop until after the end of the U.S. Civil War. The peak was recorded in 1880-1882, when a total of 324,000 Canadians entered the United States during the three-year period, and the U.S. Census of 1890 reported 980,000 persons who had been born in Canada.

Of the Canadian-born living in the U.S. in 1890, just under one-third were shown as being of French origin. At first glance, this would convey the impression that emigration has not affected the racial balance in Canada, since those leaving have been of about the same mix as those remaining. However, it should be considered that French-Canadian emigrants subtract from the irreplaceable stock, while many of the non-French were merely the children of more-or-less recent immigrants who had used Canada as a stopover point on the way from Europe to the United States; historically, Canada has retained only about half the immigrants who have landed at her ports.

Table 31

Number of French-Canadians and of Children of French-Canadians living in the United States, Censuses of 1900-1950

U.S. Census	*Immigrants*	*Children of Immigrants*	*Total*
1900	395,000	456,000	851,000
1910	385,000	563,000	948,000
1920	308,000	562,000	870,000
1930	371,000	735,000	1,106,000
1940	273,000	635,000	908,000
1950	238,000	520,000	758,000

The ebb and flow of migration southward is shown by the above table. It was in 1900 that the first-generation French-Canadians living in the United States reached a maximum; a secondary peak was recorded in 1930, just before the Depression choked off migration, but it should be noted that the 1931 Census showed 55,600 persons of French origin who had been born in the United States but who had moved up to Canada. Thus, the net loss to French Canada was far smaller in 1930 than it had been thirty years earlier, even in terms of absolute numbers; as a proportion of the total French-Canadian population, the southward migration of this century has been far less important than that of the pre-1900 decades.

As noted previously, there is no figure available from the U.S. Census to show the origin of persons born in the United States of native-born parents. However, a guess based on the figures of the above table would place the present French-Canadian-origin population of the United States at somewhere in the vicinity of 2,500,000 persons, or more than double the number of those of French origin living in Canada outside Quebec Province.

How does it happen that those who went southward seem to have entered into the mainstream of the language group they found there, while those who moved to other provinces of Canada have, to some extent at least, tended to remain apart?

One clue may be found in the census figures. Of those living in the United States at the time of the 1930 Census, over 80% were found in urban areas. The 1931 Census of Canada, however, reported that less than 40% of those of French origin outside Quebec were living in urban areas.

The two groups, those who went westward and those who migrated to the United States, have, therefore, developed under completely different circumstances. The former have, to a large extent, remained close to the land and, by living in isolated communities, have been able to preserve their language through two or three generations; they were greatly aided by the fact that they had clergy of their own language group who militantly encouraged their resistance to assimilation.

Those who went south, however, entered into established towns where they had daily contact in the streets and at the mill with their English-speaking fellow-citizens. For them, English was the language of advancement and their children were quick to learn it. Their bishops, also, had an announced policy of encouraging the use of English in the churches and in the parochial schools.

New England received the bulk of the French-Canadian immigration and Professor Theriault, of Dartmouth University, has made a detailed study of the French-origin group which constitutes half the population of Nashua, New Hampshire. He distinguishes three stages in the development of this group.*

From 1870 to 1910, there was a period of vigorous growth as newcomers poured in from Quebec. Several French-Canadian parishes were established and built their own schools, hospitals, orphanages and social clubs. French was the dominant language and English was spoken only as a second tongue.

*George F. Theriault: Chapter contributed to "Canadian Dualism" (1960).

From 1910 to 1930, the second generation continued the work of their fathers but with considerably less spirit of being French-Canadians and considerably more of being bilingual Americans. The parish priests, also, had ceased to aggressively promote the French language.

From 1930 onwards, assimilation quickened as the first and second generations died off. The third and fourth generation Franco-Americans were aware of their origin but saw no purpose in retaining a language that has no official status and very little economic value in the country in which they are now permanently settled. The Church, too, had begun to actively discourage the use of French and now appears to be only one step away from complete abolition of French-language "national parishes" and their schools.

Today, there is no language problem in New England. Assimilation has been almost complete although, as Professor Theriault emphasizes, this has not led to any significant loss of their Catholic religion by those who now speak only English.

It would be interesting to see a similar case-study published on the French-origin residents of Northern New York State, an area where there has always been close contact with Quebec Province.

In Plattsburgh, for example,which is only twenty miles south of the border and well within the range of French-language radio stations at Montreal, the church built as "Saint-Pierre" in 1891 has now become "St. Peter's"; sermons in French were discontinued as far back as 1946, when the parish priest found, with regret, that none of the younger generation could understand the language of their grandfathers. Although there is a parochial school, the only language of instruction is English.

The linguistic fate of the 2,500,000 Franco-Americans tends to undermine the argument of those who still hopefully claim that French-speaking minorities will be able to survive indefinitely in those parts of Canada lying outside the Soo-Moncton limits.

CHAPTER XII

The Atlantic Region

Although there had been Viking settlements in Newfoundland some six hundred years earlier, permanent occupation of what is now the Atlantic Region of Canada dates only from the beginning of the 17th Century, when demographic, technological and political factors finally combined to make colonization possible.

The coasts from Labrador down to New England had, of course, become very familiar to all the seafaring nations of western Europe through the voyages of their fishing boats: by the middle of the 16th Century, records show that there might be as many as 400 vessels at a time on the Grand Banks, coming from England, France, Portugal and Spain.

Almost without exception, however, the captains of these boats were concerned only with the catching of fish for the European market; to them, the North American continent was merely a convenient series of beaches on which to dry their catch and colonization was to be discouraged, since it might lead to desertions among their crews.

Thus, although the ships of Henry VII sailed around Newfoundland in 1497 and Jacques Cartier explored the St. Lawrence some forty years later, the first permanent settlement dates only from 1605, when Champlain founded Port Royal, in what is now Nova Scotia; it is interesting to note, in view of the subsequent identification of "French" and "Catholic" in North America, that these earliest French settlers were often Huguenots.

St. John's (Newfoundland) was founded in 1613 and Boston in 1630; for the next century, the history of the colonies along the Atlantic coast was to be one of almost constant conflict, with French land power pitted against British control of the sea.

French strength reached its peak during the last decade of the 17th Century when, following the repulse of Phips' attack on Quebec, French-led Abenakis ravaged the Maine coast to as far south as Kennebunk and d'Iberville wrought havoc on Newfoundland; for a brief period, the outnumbered defenders of New France held the ascendancy.

However, Port Royal was captured by a British (including New England) expedition in 1710 and, as the wars in Europe had gone badly for France, the Treaty of Utrecht (1713) reflected the victories of Marlborough by placing under British control not only the entirety of Newfoundland but, also, the territory rather loosely defined as "Acadia". France was left with Cape Breton and Prince Edward Island and also retained a disputed possession of what is now New Brunswick.

There were perhaps 4,000 Acadians in 1713, and Newfoundland's population of 3,500 included a few hundred of French origin, so the French had a slight numerical preponderance in the region as a whole. This advantage was increased when troops were sent from France to garrison the new fortress of Louisbourg.

To offset French power in Cape Breton, Halifax was founded in 1749. The original 2,544 immigrants brought by Governor Cornwallis were soon joined by fishermen and traders from New England and by settlers from Germany but, at the outbreak of hostilities in 1755, were still not numerous enough to deal with the potential threat of an uprising by the Acadians living around the Bay of Fundy. These latter were, therefore, loaded into transports and removed from the combat zone, their farms being made available to newcomers of British stock.

After the fall of Louisbourg, in 1758, and the subsequent cession of the entire Atlantic region to Britain by the Treaty of Paris, most of the garrison and many of the civilian residents of Cape Breton and of Prince Edward Island returned to France. The French population of the region was, therefore, very considerably reduced during the decade 1755-1765.

Table 32

Population of French Origin in the Maritimes, by sub-regions, 1755 and 1765

	1755	*1765*
Cape Breton Island	3,800	1,000
Other Nova Scotia	8,200	2,300
Prince Edward Island	3,000	800
New Brunswick	4,300	6,250
Total	19,300	10,350

By 1765, the non-French population of Nova Scotia was about 10,000 while that of Newfoundland was just over 15,000. Those of French origin were, therefore, outnumbered five-to-two even before heavy immigration began from New England after the Revolutionary War.

The northern half of New Brunswick is to be the subject of a separate chapter, since it was in this previously uninhabited area that most of the Acadians finally relocated. In the south of New Brunswick and in the other three Atlantic Provinces, the French language has never been of importance since 1765, a fact recognized by even the Catholic Church in 1817 when Nova Scotia was made independent of the Diocese of Quebec and given its own bishop, of Irish origin. The present position of the French-speaking population is shown by the following table.

Table 33

Population of French Mother Tongue vs. Total Population, Atlantic Region, by Provinces, 1961 Census

	Total population	*M.T. French*	*Ratio*
Newfoundland	458,000	3,150	0.7%
Prince Edward Island	105,000	7,950	7.6%
Nova Scotia	737,000	39,600	5.4%
Southern New Brunswick	261,000	11,750	4.5%
Atlantic Region	1,561,000	62,450	4.0%

Even the above figures inflate somewhat the true position of the French language in the Atlantic region, since many of those who are shown as being of French mother tongue now use English as the language of the home.

Table 34

Number of Children (aged 0-9) of French Mother Tongue vs. Number of all Mother Tongues, Nova Scotia and Prince Edward Island, Censuses of 1931-1961

	1931	*1941*	*1951*	*1961*
All languages	129,000	133,000	175,000	210,000
M. T. French	10,400	9,200	8,900	7,800
French/Total	8.0%	6.9%	5.1%	3.9%

Table 34 shows that the number of children of French mother tongue has been steadily declining during the last three decades while children of English mother tongue were twice as numerous in 1961 as they had been in 1931. This is a sure sign that an ever-increasing number of adults of French origin, the family-forming generation, are bringing up their children in English; although many of these parents will, under Census definitions, continue to be classed as "of French mother tongue", they cannot really be considered members of the French-speaking community.

At present, the future of the French language in the Atlantic region appears hardly promising; Table 9 has shown that three-quarters of those of French ethnic origin have already been assimilated and the few who still speak French are to be found chiefly in rural areas, where the general income and education level is not such as to indicate that the minorities can compensate by quality what they lack in numbers. It is not surprising, therefore, that some of the Acadian groups who testified recently before the Royal Commission were using the term "extinction". Some comments on the state of the French language in the various provinces follow:

Newfoundland

Of the 3,150 persons of French mother tongue found in the province at the time of the 1961 Census, almost 1,000 were on the mainland. As men outnumbered women by three-to-one among this group, they would appear to be chiefly transient labor from Quebec or New Brunswick, working on various projects in Labrador.

Most of those on the island were living in a small area of the west coast, around Stephenville and St. Georges Bay. Some of these were fairly recent arrivals from St. Pierre and Miquelon but most were descendants of Acadians, including some who migrated from the Magdalen Islands about 1850.

The establishment of a U.S.A.F. base at Harmon was a fatal blow to the French language in this area. For the past twenty years, those employed at the base have had to work in English, while social contacts radiating from Harmon have completely destroyed the old isolation of the fishing villages which had preserved the older generation from anglicization.

Elsewhere, there are only 614 persons who gave their mother tongue as French, including 126 at St. John's, and the influence of the French language in Newfoundland would appear to be negligible.

Nova Scotia

The French-speaking population of Nova Scotia reached a peak of over 45,000 in the early part of the present century but has suffered heavy losses through assimilation and is now back almost to its 1871 level. The distribution of this population is given by the following table.

Table 35

Population of French Mother Tongue, specified sub-regions of Nova Scotia, Census of 1871 vs. Census of 1961

	Actual number in each area		*% of total population of area*	
	1871	*1961*	*1871*	*1961*
Yarmouth & Digby	11,300	15,300	32%	35%
Richmond & Inverness	9,600	9,800	26	33
5 eastern counties	5,300	5,200	5	2
Halifax	500	5,900	2	3
Elsewhere	6,100	3,400	3	1
NOVA SCOTIA	32,800	39,600	8½%	5½%

At present, the most important concentration is that found at the westernmost end of the province; in recognition of this, the Diocese of Yarmouth was split off from Halifax in 1953 to give the Acadians of Nova Scotia a bishop of their own language.

In Cape Breton, the last part of the province to fall under British rule, those of French mother tongue are numerous in the rural counties of Richmond and Inverness but are heavily outnumbered by the English-speaking population of the cities on the Island (Sydney, Glace Bay, etc.) and their relative importance has decreased considerably as compared to that of a century ago.

The increase in the French population of Halifax is somewhat illusory. Although 5,857 persons reported that their mother tongue had been French, examination of the languages spoken by children indicates that just over 90% of the younger French ethnics have adopted English as the language of the home. It would appear that any Acadian who moves to Halifax from a rural county is accepting almost automatic assimilation.

The Census shows that those who still speak French are to be found only in rural areas where the general levels of both income and education are below average: in Digby, Richmond and Inverness Counties, the average income of adult males was less than $2,100 in 1961, as compared to a provincial average of $3,200. There is not, necessarily, a cause and effect relationship between poverty and the speaking of French, but these figures do indicate that the Acadians of Nova Scotia lack not only numbers but, also, resources; their future hardly appears bright.

Prince Edward Island

In the western end of Prince Edward Island, those of French mother tongue number 6,700 and make up 16% of the total population of Prince County. Elsewhere, there are only 1,300 scattered among 62,000 English-speaking Islanders.

The resurgence of the Acadians in New Brunswick, only a few miles away, has had some influence on their cousins in Prince Edward Island but this is weakened by the fact that the jurisdiction of the Archbishop of Moncton does not extend beyond the mainland; the Catholics of the Island have had their own bishop, usually of Irish origin, since 1829.

Assimilation is progressing rapidly, accelerated by the fact that five out of six Catholics are English-speaking, a circumstance favoring linguistically-mixed marriages. Among the younger generation of French ethnics, 68% were using English as the language of the home in 1961, as compared to only 30% in 1931; a brief presented to the Laurendeau-Dunton Commission by St. Dunstan's University commented on the deplorable state of the French language as spoken by the remainder.

Table 36

Population of French Mother Tongue vs. Total Population, Prince Edward Island, Censuses of 1881-1961

	1881	*1901*	*1941*	*1951*	*1961*
Total Population	108,891	103,000	95,000	98,000	105,000
Mother Tongue* French	10,751*	13,900*	10,700	8,500	8,000
French/Total	10%	13%	11%	9%	8%

*"Racial Origin French" in 1881 and 1901.

CHAPTER XIII

The Acadians — End of a Dream

It was the fate of the Acadians, like their counterparts in Newfoundland and Maine, to be caught between French land power and English sea power. During every formal war and several informal conflicts, New England privateers and French-led Indians ravaged the coastal settlements struggling to exist in the middle ground between New France and New England.

The climax of this drama was reached during the latter half of the 18th Century, when the Acadian population was finally uprooted and forced to move from the old homeland around the Bay of Fundy. It is seldom realized that this displacement was commenced by the French authorities, well before the eviction commemorated by Longfellow.

To protect his line of defence along what is now the Nova Scotia-New Brunswick boundary, the French commander, LaCorne, decided to establish a zone of "scorched earth" in front of Fort Beauséjour. In 1750, this policy was implemented, when LeLoutre burned the church and village of Beaubassin and forced the several thousand inhabitants of the region to move westward, to new lands around what is now Moncton.

Deportation to the south, in a series of removals between 1755 and 1762, was the fate of most of the remaining Acadians in Nova Scotia, as Governor Lawrence took what he considered to be the necessary precautions against potential fifth-columnists. A quarter-century later, those who had been living in southwestern New Brunswick were pushed up the Saint John River, into Madawaska, to make room for some ten thousand Loyalists who arrived at the end of the Revolutionary War.

Many of the Acadians returned from exile after 1765, but their lands had been occupied by settlers of British stock and they were forced to establish a new homeland along the East Coast of New Brunswick. Here, they took root and, like their cousins in Madawaska, began to increase in number.

By the end of the 18th Century, a linguistic division of the province had been established, which persists to this day. North of a line drawn from

Madawaska to Moncton, the 1961 Census found some 200,000 persons of French mother tongue; south of this line, there were only 11,753, including 6,037 within Saint John.

At the time of Confederation, almost two-thirds of the population of New Brunswick lived in the predominantly-English southern counties. During the next sixty years, however, emigration held the population of the south almost unchanged while that of the northern counties more than doubled, in part due to the employment created by pulp mills and other industries established during the period.

Table 37

Population of New Brunswick, North vs. South, Censuses of 1871-1961

	1871	*1901*	*1931*	*1951*	*1961*
North	105,000	154,000	226,000	296,000	336,000
South	181,000	177,000	182,000	219,000	262,000

Within the north, the growth of the French-speaking element was greater than that of the population as a whole. From 42,000 in 1871, the Acadians of this region (reinforced, in Madawaska and Restigouche Counties, by some net migration from Quebec Province) grew to 77,000 in 1901 and to 130,000 in 1931. By 1951 there were 177,000 persons of French mother tongue in the North and an additional 8,000 in the South.

The results of the 1951 Census came as a great encouragement to those who dreamed of an "Acadie" restored through the cradle. Not only did this census show 36% of the total population of the province to be French-speaking, but further analysis revealed that this was the first language of 45% of the school-age population, the citizens of the future. Even disinterested observers were predicting that New Brunswick would soon have a French-speaking majority, probably by 1981.

The increase in their number had been accompanied by improvements in the facilities available to the Acadians. Writing in 1961, the Rector of St. Joseph University listed: "A daily newspaper, French-language radio and television, modern schools, diocesan organization surpassing the hopes of those of former generations (creation of the Archdiocese of Moncton, etc.) and a greater intellectual maturity"; this list could have been extended, in 1963, when the legislature voted to establish a French-language university at Moncton.

However, the sheer rate of growth of the Acadian population led to its downfall. Three-quarters of the French-speaking population of New

Brunswick were to be found in rural areas in 1951 and the increasing mechanization of logging and farming has resulted in these traditional industries being unable to absorb all those who reach majority each year; when competing for the new types of employment available, Acadian applicants are often at a serious disadvantage due to weaknesses in their educational records.

The extent to which the French-speaking population of New Brunswick has lagged behind those of other origins is demonstrated by the figures of the following table, taken from the 1951 Census. This gives the proportion, among persons who are no longer attending school, of those who have completed the specified number of years: it is apparent that only one Acadian in five had completed even the first year of high school while almost half the English-speaking population had reached or passed that level.

Table 38

Percentage having completed specified number of Years of School, among those no longer at School, Population of French Origin vs. that of non-French Origins, New Brunswick, 1951 Census

Years completed	*French Origin*	*Other Origins*
1-4	24%	6½%
5-8	56	46
9-12	18	42
13-16	1½	4½
over 16	½	1

The low level of education among the French-speaking population has tended to restrict them to farming and other subsistence occupations. This sets in motion a cycle: the average income in predominantly-French districts is too low to support a local tax rate adequate to pay for the schools required for the typically numerous children (Gloucester County is, at present, under provincial tutelage after defaulting on bank loans contracted to pay school expenses) so the level of education among those of French mother tongue tends to drop ever further behind that of the English-speaking population, giving the latter a clear advantage when competing for what jobs are available.

The consequence is that, in recent years, emigration from New Brunswick has been much higher among the Acadians than among the

English-speaking population. As the following table shows, 41 % of those who were aged 5-14 in 1941 had disappeared from the province by 1961; it would appear from the figures that they move out as soon as they reach their majority, to seek a source of livelihood elsewhere.

Table 39

Number of Persons of French and of non-French Origins, born 1927-1936, enumerated in New Brunswick at Census of 1941 vs. Censuses of 1951 and 1961

	1941	*1951*	*1961*	*1941-1961 loss*
French Origin	20,547	16,007	12,208	—41 %
Other Origins	27,586	22,298	21,385	—22 %

The 1961 Census, therefore, brought a rude awakening to those who had dreamed of Acadian supremacy. During a decade in which the total population of the province had risen by 82,000, those of French mother tongue had shown a net increase of only 25,000 and their relative strength had actually fallen, to 35 % among the population as a whole and to 38 % among those of school age.

However, it is not only in numbers that the position of the Acadians has deteriorated. As outlined above, the economic future of those who have retained the French language is hardly bright. Like their neighbors in the Gaspé and Lower St. Lawrence regions of Quebec, they seem to be doomed to stagnation while the more promising of their young people depart to seek their fortunes elsewhere.

In Quebec, the "colonization parishes" and other poverty-stricken rural areas can be kept alive through transfer of tax revenues collected at Montreal; the fact that the rural counties elect a disproportionate number of members to the Legislative Assembly plays its part in encouraging this game of Robin Hood.

In New Brunswick, however, the political picture is complicated by the language split. Of the 26 Conservatives elected at the 1967 vote, not one is an Acadian and, with a solitary exception, all represent ridings located south of the Edmundston-Moncton line. Mr. Robichaud's support comes almost entirely from the northern counties, although it must be noted that 13 of the 32 Liberal members are of non-French origins.

It would appear, therefore, that language barriers and cultural prejudices still tend to prevent a common front being formed between rural voters in the north and those in the south, despite the similarity of their economic interests. As a consequence, it is only within the past two years that even the first steps have been taken toward improvement of rural facilities at the expense of the urban taxpayer.

Until now, for example, provincial school grants have been contributed only on a matching basis, relative to the taxes collected locally; this has meant that the amount of such aid, per pupil, has been least in those Acadian districts where the need was actually the greatest. Not surprisingly, this was one of the first fields for application of the "Equal Opportunity" program of the present government.

However, despite the changes that are being made in provincial policy and regardless of the amount of federal aid poured into the northern counties through A.R.D.A., economic pressure will continue to work against the French language. The old days of unskilled manpower and subsistence living standards are passing; the increasing demand for material well-being tends to reduce the French-speaking population because:

1) Many Acadians are leaving New Brunswick to seek employment elsewhere; this removes from the province not only the young adults but, also, their future children;

2) Others are drifting to the cities of their own province, where the tendency toward assimilation is much higher than in rural areas; and

3) Those who remain in rural areas may tend to postpone marriage, as occurred in French Canada generally during the Depression years, or to adopt other measures that will reduce the number of children born.

Although there is no clear trend with regard to the postponement of marriages, out-migration has had a role of major importance in reducing the rate of natural increase of the French-speaking population of New Brunswick, since those who leave the province tend to be in the child-bearing age groups.

In 1941, there had been just over 31,000 female children (aged 0-14) of French origin in the province. In 1961, however, there were only 20,000 women of French origin in the corresponding age bracket (20-34), so it would appear that out-migration of Acadian women has been almost as heavy as that reported for their men (see Table 39). It should be noted that the 1951 Census had reported 21,000 women of French origin aged 20-34, so the child-bearing population actually diminished in numbers during the decade.

The above figures were for the entire province. If we look only at the three counties (Gloucester, Kent and Madawaska) in which 87% of the population is of French mother tongue, a trend becomes strikingly apparent:

live births in these counties had totalled 4,596 in 1950 but declined steadily thereafter, 3,897 being reported in 1960 and 3,282 in 1965, the last year for which figures are available. This is a drop of 29% in 15 years. The four mixed counties had also experienced a decline in births during this period but the eight predominantly-English counties saw births increase from 5,876 in 1950 to 6,706 in 1964, before dropping off to 6,121 in 1965.

If this trend continues, then the birth rates of the two language groups will approach equality. Meanwhile, assimilation (increasing as the old rural isolation disappears) and out-migration are working against the French language.

There is, of course, no serious likelihood that the Acadians will disappear overnight. On the contrary, they will probably continue, possibly indefinitely, to predominate in Gloucester, Kent and Madawaska Counties (Restigouche is less certain).

However, the peak of their relative numerical importance appears to have passed and there is now little expectation of their ever outnumbering the English-speaking residents of the province. The dream, nourished for so many decades and, seemingly, so close to realization in 1951, has now ended.

CHAPTER XIV

L'Etat de Québec

Sixty years after the end of French rule, Quebec was English-speaking to a degree hardly imaginable today. The French-speaking population of the colony numbered less than half a million and were almost all living along the St. Lawrence, while those of British origin were in undisputed majority in the Eastern Townships, the Ottawa Valley and at Montreal.

The first attempts to establish English-speaking settlements had not been successful, the sites chosen being, usually, along the St. Lawrence below Quebec City (Rivière-du-Loup was called "Fraserville" until 1919). However, large-scale immigration began in 1784, when Philipsburg was founded by Loyalists coming up through Vermont.

Further waves of neutral but land-hungry New Englanders followed and fanned out into the whole area of the Eastern Townships, from Lake Megantic to Huntingdon. After a road had been built from Quebec City to Lennoxville, in 1815, these original settlers were joined by Irish and Scottish immigrants; others settled in the Ottawa Valley and in the Laurentians north of Montreal and Quebec, where names such as Shawbridge and Stoneham may still be found on the map.

These settlements, with the Scottish counties of Eastern Ontario, formed a ring around the old French parishes, while citizens of British origins dominated the economic life of Quebec City and actually outnumbered the French-Canadian population at Montreal.

By 1837, one Quebec resident in four was English-speaking, a very impressive increase from the 200 families reported in 1764. However, most of this gain had been achieved through immigration from the United States or from the British Isles; the former virtually ceased early in the 19th Century and the latter began to decline with the opening of lands further west.

Unlike Quebec, which had grown around the natural line of communication provided by the St. Lawrence, Ontario had to wait for the construction of canals and railways before its economic potential could be realized. Once these had been built, the expansion of Upper Canada was almost explosive: between 1851 and 1871, the area of improved land more than doubled and the population rose from 952,000 to 1,621,000.

Since the middle of the 19th Century, the cities of Quebec Province have served mainly as ports of entry for immigrants proceeding further into the continent. The following table shows the extent to which Ontario has been the favored destination during the past century.

Table 40

Number of Persons born outside Canada enumerated in Ontario and in Quebec, Censuses of 1851-1961

	1851	*1871*	*1901*	*1931*	*1961*
Ontario	399,000	441,000	324,000	798,000	1,353,000
Quebec	95,000	77,000	89,000	247,000	388,000

The growth of Ontario to its present position as the most populous province is due to these immigrants and to their Canadian-born children and grandchildren; had a greater number remained in Quebec, the entire linguistic and political picture of Canada would have been changed.

This westward drift of population is still visible today. According to Hansard (April 20, 1966), 240,432 immigrants entered Quebec during the 10 years 1946-1955; of these, only 126,325 were still living in that province at the time of the 1961 Census. The consequence is that there has been a long-term downward trend in the relative importance of Quebec's non-French population.

Table 41

French-speaking and non-French Populations of Quebec Province, Censuses of 1837-1961

	1837	*1871*	*1901*	*1931*	*1961*
		(figures are in thousands of persons)			
French	434	930	1,322	2,270	4,270
Others	166	262	327	604	989
Others/Total	28%	22%	20%	21%	19%

Looking at the figures of the above table, it will be noticed that the rate of increase of the French-speaking population has been far from steady.

Although the non-French element of Quebec's population has been weakened by out-migration, the same factor has affected the French-Canadians at various times, particularly during the period 1871-1901, when the southward movement into New England reached its peak.

Table 42

Rate of Growth* of the French-speaking Population of Quebec Province, for specified periods between 1760 and 1961

Period	*1760-1837*	*1837-1871*	*1871-1901*	*1901-1931*	*1931-1941*	*1941-1951*	*1951-1961*
Rate	2.5%	2.3%	1.2%	1.8%	1.8%	2.1%	2.5%

*Rate compounded annually.

During the two centuries under review, there was a rapid initial growth as surplus population expanded outwards from the old parishes along the St. Lawrence and gradually filled up the more remote regions of the province. By the middle of the 19th Century, the rate of natural increase had fallen off slightly (largely due to epidemics, in the 1830's and 1840's, caused by immigrants) but there was still very little movement out of the province, probably not more than a few hundred families crossing the river to settle in Prescott and Russell Counties of Eastern Ontario.

Southward emigration became important during the latter half of the 19th Century and the full effects of the New England hemorrhage can be seen in the low rate of growth of Quebec's French-speaking population between 1871 and 1901; the outward movement continued, at a somewhat reduced rate, until 1930.

Economic factors, forcing postponement of marriage and other family-limiting measures, held down natural increase during the Depression years; the reaction, during two decades of wartime and postwar prosperity, brought the rate of increase back up to the level reported for the early years of the colony.

This does not mean, of course, that conditions are still the same as they were two centuries ago. However, the lower birth rates of the 1950's were accompanied by a correspondingly lower death rate, as living conditions improved and as medical care was made available to the mass of the population.

There is now little room for improvement in the death rate, so this factor can be regarded as stable. Movements of population are unpredictable, but it would seem that there is very little net migration of French-speakers across the Quebec border at present, those who leave the province being more or less balanced by new arrivals from the Maritimes, Ontario and Europe.

Unless the migration picture changes radically, in one direction or the other, the only variable left to affect the future growth of the French-speaking population of Quebec will be the birth rate.

Birth rates have been discussed, in some detail, in previous chapters; in the latter part of "La Revanche des Berceaux", we have noted that births registered in Quebec, for families of all origins, are currently at an annual level of only 104,000, as compared to the average of 140,000 for each of the years 1956-1960. This means that the rate of natural increase, for the entire population of Quebec, is down to only 1.1% per annum.

Had birth rates continued at the 1941-1961 level, then there would have been almost ten million French-Canadians living in Quebec by the end of this century, a rather frightening prospect for those who would have had to provide the necessary educational and employment opportunities; it is hardly surprising that at least some politicians have expressed satisfaction with the present downward trend in family size.

However, there are still major problems to be faced. Twenty years ago, there were only 60,000 persons of French mother tongue reaching their majority annually in Quebec. The figure is, currently, about 95,000 and will rise to 110,000 by 1981. Employment must be found for these new citizens, very few of whom will be able or willing to make their living in the once-favored rural occupations.

Table 43

French-speaking Population of Quebec Province, Rural vs. Urban, Censuses of 1871-1961

		1871	*1901*	*1931*	*1961*
Urban	Montreal	85,000	231,000	605,000	1,366,000
	Other	100,000	243,000	720,000	1,673,000
Rural	non-farm	745,000	848,000	953,000	701,000
	on farms				534,000

Three-quarters of the French-speaking population of Quebec is now to be found in urban areas and only one in eight has remained on the farm. As agriculture and logging become increasingly mechanized, the amount of manpower required in these industries will drop, so the depopulation of the rural parishes will be accelerated by economic pressure.

How well is the average French-Canadian prepared for survival in this new economy? The answer appears to be that his training has lagged far behind that received by English-speaking Canadians.

Table 44

Percentage Attending School of Population aged 15-19, Quebec, New Brunswick and Ontario, Censuses of 1931-1961

	1931	*1941*	*1951*	*1961*
Quebec	23.6%	25.2%	26.9%	50.1%
New Brunswick	31.4	32.4	40.6	56.7
Ontario	37.4	36.1	43.6	65.8

As can be seen, the average school-leaving age in Quebec has been lower than in the two neighboring provinces and the comparison would be even more unfavorable had the figures for English-speaking children not bolstered the Quebec average. This is, of course, a consequence of the traditional French-Canadian philosophy of education discussed in a previous chapter: that only a very small "élite" should be given the opportunity to proceed past elementary school.

Addressing the 1965 meeting of the "Institut canadien des affaires publiques", the vice-dean of social sciences of the Université de Montréal stated bluntly that the general level of education among French-Canadians had actually deteriorated during the previous seventy years. The program on which the Liberals were swept into power in 1960 stressed this same theme, that education in Quebec needed a complete overhaul.

It is, therefore, only within the past few years that there has been any serious effort to educate the masses in French Canada. The ultimate goal is that the needs of Quebec industry and government may, eventually, be met from among her own French-speaking population; whether this goal can be attained will depend on the success of Mr. Gérin-Lajoie's successors in finding the teachers and finances to continue the work so recently started.

The purpose of Confederation was to permit each language group to develop fully within the province or provinces in which that group was in the majority. That the French-speaking population of Quebec had, until quite recently, not availed itself fully of the powers granted by the B.N.A. Act, is often blamed upon the great influence wielded by the English-speaking minority; one former editor of Le Devoir went so far as to postulate the theory of "Le Roi nègre", that the then premier was merely a puppet obeying the commands of the English-speaking capitalists who controlled the province's economy and whose contributions to campaign funds could decide the results of an election.

Such machinations, if they existed, were carried out in a discreet manner and French-Canadians have held most of the political titles in Quebec for many decades. As far back as 1914, the custom ceased of electing, alternately, English- and French-speaking mayors of Montreal; at the provincial level, minority representation has been notoriously low in the cabinet and it is quite unthinkable that the premier should be other than a French-Canadian.

However, it is only within the past six years that a serious effort has been made by the Quebec legislature to exercise all the powers that it has possessed since 1867. Under Premier Lesage, taxes were levied on the citizens of both language groups to build schools for the French-speaking masses and to purchase, either directly or through the Société générale de Financement, industries in which French will become, to use the euphemism coined by a recent Minister of Cultural Affairs, "la langue prioritaire".

The infrastructure is, therefore, already in place. If the universities of French Canada can meet the challenge now laid upon them, if they can turn out administrators and professional men in numbers sufficient to satisfy the needs of government and business as well as of the many new schools, then, but only then, will Quebec become a truly French-speaking province.

CHAPTER XV

Quebec's Forgotten Fifth

As the French-speaking population increases in numbers and in influence, what is happening to the English-speaking minority in Quebec, a group which, for almost two centuries, dominated the economic life of the province and whose members still include many of the key personnel in industry and commerce?

During the past hundred years, there has been a great change in the linguistic complexion of Quebec. No longer is English the only language heard in the Eastern Townships and the Ottawa Valley. No longer are English-speaking citizens in the majority at Montreal, as they were until 1865, and the few still to be found at Quebec City give no indication of the pre-Confederation strength of the English language in La Vieille Capitale.

Although the non-French element still represented 19% of Quebec's total population in 1961, a relatively small drop from the 22% reported in 1871, a breakdown of these figures shows that the English-speaking minority is disappearing from many parts of the province and now flourishes only in the metropolitan area of Montreal.

Table 45

Non-French Populations, Montreal vs. Other Parts of Quebec Province, Censuses of 1871-1961

	1871	*1901*	*1931*	*1961*
Montreal	57,000	129,000	399,000	743,000
Elsewhere	205,000	198,000	205,000	246,000
Montreal/Total	22%	40%	66%	75%

Those of the minority who remain outside Montreal are occasionally to be found on the land, the survivors of those English-speaking pioneers who opened up so many areas of the province during the early decades of British rule. This is particularly noticeable in the Eastern Townships, the Ottawa Valley and the Gaspé Peninsula, although there are smaller colonies along the southern fringe of the Laurentians and elsewhere.

However, the English language is losing ground in all the rural areas, as the younger generation moves away to seek a better living elsewhere. Those of British origin living in rural Quebec declined from 160,000 in 1871 to 130,000 in 1901 and to 93,000 in 1931; the 1961 figure of 85,000 in rural areas included only 26,000 who were actually on farms.

Most of the English-speaking population of Quebec is, therefore, to be found in urban areas. Many of those living outside Montreal are working in the paper mills and chemical plants of the St. Maurice Valley, in the aluminum or pulp industries of Lake St. John, in the iron industry of the Lower North Shore or in the mines and mills of Abitibi-Temiscamingue.

A striking feature of this English-speaking population is that relatively few of the adults were born within the Province of Quebec. The 1961 Census showed that some 45% of the non-French adults living in Quebec had been born outside Canada; many of the others had come from Ontario, the Maritimes or the Western Provinces (in that order), attracted by the recruiting efforts of industries unable to find sufficient trained personnel among the locally-born.

(Unfortunately, the Census no longer breaks down interprovincial migration by language groups. In 1941, the last year for which such figures are available, one-sixth of the Canadian-born, English-speaking population of Quebec had come from other provinces, chiefly Ontario; this was for the population of all ages, so well over one-sixth of the adults would have been born in other provinces.)

As a consequence, there is a considerable volatility to the non-French population of Quebec. It is not improbable that any strong trend toward imposition of French as the language of work within the province would have, as a consequence, the massive outward migration of those who prefer to work in English. As a possible precedent for such an exodus, it may be of interest to examine the history of one group who have already, to a large extent, departed.

At the time of Confederation, Quebec citizens of Irish origin (most of whom were Catholics) had been sufficiently numerous that government appointments were often allotted on the basis: one Irish, one Anglo-Protestant and four French.

Since that time, however, those who reported their origin as Irish have been slipping in importance to such an extent that they are now hardly more numerous than such recent immigrants as the Italians and the Jews; the story is told by the following table.

Table 46

Ethnic Origins of the non-French Population, as Percentages of the Total Population of Quebec Province, Censuses of 1871-1961

	1871	*1901*	*1921*	*1941*	*1961*
Irish	10.4%	7.0%	4.0%	3.3%	2.5%
English	5.9	7.0	8.3	7.5	6.1
Scottish	4.2	3.6	2.7	2.7	2.1
All others	1.7	2.2	4.9	5.6	8.7

Some care must be taken when interpreting the figures of the above table, since many Irish immigrants intermarried with French-Canadians and the descendants of some of these marriages have been assimilated to such an extent that they no longer think to give their true origin to the Census enumerator. However, the downward trend in the Irish group appears far too strong to be explained by this factor alone; despite some immigration and a birth rate intermediate between those of the French and of the English, the Irish-origin population of Quebec declined from a peak of 124,000 in 1881 to only 95,000 in 1921.

It seems probable, therefore, that there was selective emigration from the province during the decades around the turn of the century. The economic and social factors that would have promoted this are quite similar to those now being felt, increasingly, by the present-day English-speaking residents of Quebec.

At the time of the 1871 Census, the "Habitant" was still close to the land and fewer than 20% of the French-origin population of Quebec was to be found in urban areas. In sharp contrast, the same census showed the Irish to have been the most heavily urbanized of the major ethnic groups; many were quite recent immigrants and these, being often without capital or education, tended to hold jobs at the lower end of the social scale.

The last third of the 19th Century, however, was a time of great change as the Industrial Revolution came to North America and upset the old ways of life. Hundreds of thousands of French-Canadians went to the mill towns of New England, but almost as many flooded into the cities and towns of their own country.

As can be seen from the table below, the urban population of French origin increased from 185,000 in 1871 to 474,000 in 1901 and more than doubled again during the subsequent twenty years. This heavy flow of population into the cities tended to saturate the labor market, keeping down the wage rates for unskilled work; the French-Canadian might accept such rates, because he had no alternative if he wished to bring up his children in his own language, but the Irish faced no similar language barrier and many would have left the province to seek their fortunes elsewhere.

Table 47

Number of Persons of Specified Ethnic Origins in Urban Areas of Quebec Province, Censuses of 1871-1961

	1871	*1901*	*1921*	*1941*	*1961*
Irish	44,500	58,900	58,100	80,300	105,000
Other British	38,800	101,400	202,000	282,000	378,000
French	185,000	474,000	969,000	1,588,000	3,009,000
All Others	3,800	19,800	94,000	160,000	415,000

Because persons of English origin were, more frequently, in occupations for which the newcomers from rural Quebec were not qualified, they were not subjected to the same competitive pressures and were able to stay and to prosper. Thanks to the high quality of the English-language school system, their children, also, were assured a favored position.

It is only within the past two decades that the English language has ceased to confer an automatic advantage on those seeking employment. The change was first noticeable in those positions which involved contact with the general public but appears to be spreading to an ever-widening range of occupations.

As French-Canadians with the necessary training and experience become available, they are being hired in preference to candidates of other mother tongues. The employer has several reasons for adopting such a policy: not only will he improve his public image (an important factor when dealing with the public; equally important when the company is in the natural resources field and must obtain leases and other concessions from the provincial government) but he will, also, save money in the long run, since recruiting is less expensive when non-monetary advantages are of importance to the new employee.

There will, of course, be no overnight displacement of all non-French personnel. Many years must elapse before French Canada will be able to provide even the barest minimum of skilled personnel for the province's needs. All too evident are the cumulative effects of a century of under-education; figures published in 1965 showed that three-quarters of the engineers in Quebec industry were English-speaking and the situation would be similar in many other professional and managerial groups.

From time to time, politicians, particularly of the more extreme splinter parties, demand that action be taken by the Quebec Legislature to abolish English-language schools or to otherwise harass the minority; it is quite unlikely that any provincial government would seriously consider introducing such measures.

This reluctance to mount a direct attack on the English language is usually attributed to the fact that Quebec is under a legal obligation to be bilingual (Section 133 of the British North America Act of 1867); such an explanation is hardly convincing, when it is considered that the legislature of Manitoba was quite capable of circumventing an identically-worded obligation imposed upon that province when it entered the confederation.

A more realistic reason, sufficient to deter even the most "nationalistic" of governments, is that the economic life of Quebec would virtually cease if the English-speaking population moved away before the schools and universities of the province could produce sufficient French-Canadians trained to take their place.

To keep Quebec's industry alive, to provide employment for the mass of the French-speaking population, it is necessary to make the non-French personnel feel at home in even the most remote mill town; this means that they and their families must be provided with schools, churches and other conveniences, paid for by either the government or by their employers (it might be noted, in this regard, that the English-language television station at Quebec City is a private venture; French-speaking minorities in Southern Ontario and elsewhere do not have similar amenities, largely because industry has no incentive to subsidize them).

It is still possible, therefore, to work and to live, quite comfortably, in Quebec without having to speak more than the occasional word of French. However, the Quiet Revolution dates only from the Fall of 1959 and its full effects will not be felt for another decade or two: will the two language groups continue to co-exist peacefully in the new Quebec, after the present educational and other reforms have born their fruit, or will those who prefer to work in English simply pack their bags and move out of the province?

Even if there is no actual exodus of those who are now working in Quebec and whose mobility is hampered by such considerations as job seniority and real estate ownership, what of the younger generation? Where will they look for employment as they complete their schooling? With an entire continent open, how many will choose to make their future in the one small corner of that continent where their mother tongue constitutes an impediment to advancement?

CHAPTER XVI

Whence the British are Gone

As mentioned in the previous chapter, there has been an actual decline in numbers of the non-French population in many parts of Quebec Province during the century since Confederation. This is particularly noticeable in the rural areas, where the old churches and the names in the cemeteries of many villages seem to have no relationship to the present population.

From the five tables of this chapter, it will be seen that the gradual disappearance of Quebec's minority is attributable to an actual departure of those who prefer to speak English. This is quite different to what has happened in all the other provinces (except Northern New Brunswick), where the fading-away of the French-speaking minorities is due to assimilation, rather than to any outward migration of those of French origin.

Our first table shows the geographical distribution of the non-French population of Quebec as it was in 1871, just after Confederation, and as it appeared at the most recent census. This table is by ethnic origins, but the 1961 figure for "of non-French origins" (230,000) was very close to that for "of English mother tongue" (203,000), due to the concentration at Montreal of most of those residents of Quebec whose origins are other than British or French.

In the following pages we shall discuss the changes that have occurred, over the past century, in the ethno-linguistic complexion of the first four sub-regions of table 48, in which the non-French represented at least one-fifth of the total population at the time of Confederation.

It should be noted that "Eastern Townships" in the following table refers to only the seven counties above the Vermont border. "Southwest" includes the five counties between the Ottawa River and the New York border, excluding towns that are suburbs of Montreal. All other counties south of the St. Lawrence are included in "South Central". "North Central" includes the St. Maurice Valley and the Laurentians.

Table 48

Population of non-French Origins, specified sub-regions of Quebec Province outside Montreal, Census of 1871 vs. Census of 1961*

	Actual Number in each area		*Strength in each area*	
	1871	*1961*	*1871*	*1961*
Eastern Townships	59,000	52,000	61%	18%
Ottawa Valley	37,000	49,000	55	23
Gaspé Peninsula	11,000	14,000	36	13
Quebec City area	26,000	19,000	20	4
Southwest	20,000	17,000	29	16
South Central	30,000	21,000	9	3
North Central	11,000	22,000	5	4
Lower St. Lawrence, South	3,000	3,000	3	1
do, North Shore	1,000	10,000	12	12
Abitibi	—	16,000	—	10
Lake St. John	—	7,000	2	3
Total	198,000	230,000	18.9%	7.3%

*Figures exclude Indians, 7,000 in 1871 and 17,000 in 1961.

The Eastern Townships:

The area on both sides of the present border between Quebec and Vermont had been unoccupied at the end of the French regime and was settled, from the South, only during the last forty years of the 18th Century. After 1783, Loyalists and other New Englanders crossed the border, in large numbers, to take up the lands being offered in the Eastern Townships by the Crown and by private land companies.

After 1815, a new element was added to the population of the area, as roads were built from Quebec City and immigrants landing at that port were encouraged to proceed southward. However, English and Gaelic continued to be the only languages spoken; a census of the Eastern Townships, taken in 1831, found only a few hundred French-Canadians among a total population of over 42,000.

This situation began to change in the 1840's, as population pressure in the older French parishes along the St. Lawrence began to drive the younger men south. By what was, perhaps, a happy coincidence, this migration coincided with an exodus from the Townships of many of the older stock, who were leaving to seek better lands in the newly-opened areas further west.

The map on page 28 illustrates the gradual penetration of the Townships by French-speaking newcomers. At the 1901 Census, the only counties south of the St. Lawrence still showing English-speaking majorities were Brome and Stanstead, along the Vermont border, and Huntingdon, in the angle between New York State and Ontario; by 1961, Brome was the sole survivor and only by a narrow margin.

The following table gives the figures for the seven counties forming a rough semi-circle above the Vermont border, the inner core of the Townships.

Table 49

Population of French, of British and of Other Origins, Seven Inner Counties* of the Eastern Townships, Censuses of 1871-1961

Origin	*1871*	*1901*	*1931*	*1961*
French	37,500	77,400	121,200	230,400
British	54,300	56,800	45,800	43,500
Other	4,500	3,000	2,700	7,500

*Brome, Compton, Missisquoi, Richmond, Shefford, Sherbrooke and Stanstead.

As can be seen, there has been a remarkable abandonment of the area by those of British origins, as also by many of the German/Dutch who represented 3,700 of the "Other Origins" in 1871. However, there would appear to have been very little net assimilation, in either direction, since persons of French mother tongue numbered 229,444 at the last census, a figure almost identical to the total of 230,354 reported for those of French origin.

In 1865, it was the then member for Brome, Christopher Dunkin, who voiced most strongly the fear that the English-speaking citizens of Lower Canada would be the ones to suffer if Confederation were to be enacted and political power put into the hands of the French majority in Quebec. By an interesting coincidence, it was again a member for Brome, Glen Brown, who felt obliged to invoke Section 80 of the B. N. A. Act, in 1962, to prevent the disappearance, from the Legislative Assembly, of the last representation of the English-speaking minority living south-east of Montreal. However, his was merely a last rear-guard action, and the English voice is becoming increasingly faint in the administration of Quebec.

The Ottawa Valley:

Although the Ottawa River was used as a route to the Upper Lakes, the Valley was still unoccupied at the end of French rule. However, timber became of commercial value during the early years of the 19th Century, attracting New England entrepreneurs: a sawmill was built at Hawkesbury in 1804 and others at Hull shortly afterward. Meanwhile, Scottish settlers had filled up the Ontario side of the Lower Ottawa and were advancing into Argenteuil County, on the Quebec side.

Irish immigrants came to work in the sawmills and logging camps, but they were soon being displaced by French-Canadians from Montreal and Vaudreuil; the fights between the two groups perpetuated the memory of such men as Jos Montferrand, who drove the Irish out of many "shanties" and became a folk-hero among those of his own language group.

In contrast to the violence further upriver, French occupation of the area around Montebello was accomplished by more peaceful means. The Petite Nation Seigneurie had been purchased by Papineau in 1801 and was deliberately colonized, the population, almost entirely French-speaking, growing to 3,000 in 1851 and to double that figure by 1867. However, at the time of Confederation, the Ottawa Valley, as a whole, still showed an English-speaking majority and its three ridings were among those specially fixed by Section 80 of the British North America Act.

This majority soon disappeared, as shown by the figures of the following table.

Table 50

Population of French, of British and of Other Origins, Argenteuil, Papineau, Hull, Gatineau and Pontiac Counties, Censuses of 1871-1961

Origin	*1871*	*1901*	*1931*	*1961*
French	28,600	71,400	93,300	166,000
British	35,500	42,200	35,300	39,500
Others	1,900	4,200	4,700	8,100

The 1961 Census showed that English was the mother tongue of the majority only in Pontiac County, where the population is quite isolated from the rest of Quebec Province and is in close contact with the English-predominant Ontario towns just across the river. Argenteuil and Gatineau were still about 30% English-speaking but Papineau and Hull were 85-90% French.

In the Ottawa Valley, we have found the same pattern as in the Eastern Townships, with a noticeable departure of the descendants of those who came from the United States or Britain to open up this region in the early part of the 19th Century. Of the 39,500 persons of British origin living in the Valley in 1961, 11,600 were residents of the Quebec-side suburbs of Ottawa and a further 8,400 were in Pontiac County; had it not been for the influence of the Ontario cities, the "British" figures of Table 50 would have shown a decline similar to that found in Table 49.

The Gaspé Peninsula:

Although Jacques Cartier landed at Gaspé during his 1534 voyage, it was not until the end of the 18th Century that settlement began. The first arrivals were Loyalists, soon followed by the ubiquitous Irish and, an unusual feature, by immigrants from the Channel Islands.

A few Acadians, returning from exile, also settled on the Chaleur coast at this time and a Father Bourg arrived at Carleton in 1786 to become Grand Vicar to the entire Acadian area (including New Brunswick). However, it was not until a century later that French-Canadians began to arrive in any numbers, some moving down the St. Lawrence while others came via the Matapedia Valley, after the railway had been completed in 1872.

In recent decades, the peninsula has been an area of heavy outward migration; due to the greater ease with which they can find employment elsewhere, this has affected the English-speaking young people more than those from French families and the population of British origin has actually declined at each census since 1931.

Table 51

Population of French, of British and of Other Origins, Bonaventure and Gaspé Counties, Censuses of 1871-1961

Origin	*1871*	*1901*	*1931*	*1961*
French	19,700	39,800	60,600	89,200
British	10,900	14,300	16,300	13,600
Others	900	1,100	1,200	2,000

Quebec City:

For over two centuries, Quebec was not only the administrative centre but, also, the main port of entry for Canada. However, by 1857, vessels from overseas were proceeding up the recently-deepened St. Lawrence to Montreal and construction of a railway system centred on that metropolis virtually killed the commercial life of Quebec just as the government was moving to Ottawa and the Imperial garrisons were being withdrawn.

At the 1861 Census, Quebec City had a population of 60,000, as compared to 90,000 for Montreal. Ten years later, Quebec's population had actually decreased slightly, to 59,700, while Montreal's had increased to 107,000. (Toronto, during the same decade, had grown from 45,000 to 56,000). The last part of the 19th Century was a period of stagnation for the Vieille Capitale, virtually without industries and reduced to living off the Provincial and Ecclesiastical establishments.

Due to their greater mobility, many of the English-speaking population abandoned the city during this time, to seek their fortunes elsewhere. From 20,000 at the date of Confederation, the non-French among Quebec City's population had dwindled to only 11,800 by the end of the 19th Century.

Table 52

Population of French, of British and of Other Origins, Quebec City and County, Censuses of 1871-1961

Origin	*1871*	*1901*	*1931*	*1951*	*1961*
French	55,600	75,700	157,000	237,000	310,000
British	22,800	13,700	12,100	13,200	14,700
Others	900	1,500	2,200	2,900	6,400

The entire county has been included in the above table, since less than half the population of British origin was living within the actual City of Quebec in 1961. Most of the others were residents of the suburbs but a few hundred were still to be found in isolated rural communities north of the city, where predominantly-Irish immigrants had established pioneer settlements in the early 19th Century.

Within the metropolitan area of Quebec, assimilation has been heavily in favor of the French language. If we exclude from our calculations the suburbs of Ste. Foy and Sillery, then the 1961 Census found 25% fewer persons of non-French mother tongues than of non-French origins (in the two upper-income suburbs excluded, there was less than 6% difference between the mother tongue and origin figures).

An increasing emphasis on the use of the French language in private industry, as well as in the recently-nationalized power companies, and its absolute priority in the provincial civil service may well lead to a complete disappearance of the other language group, whose members once made up more than one-third of the city's population and who completely dominated its economic life.

CHAPTER XVII

Montreal — The Two Solitudes

When Hugh MacLennan wrote his well-known novel, it was natural that the setting should have been Montreal, that polyglot metropolis in which each of Canada's two major language groups has formed its own isolated communities.

To the French geographer, Professor Raoul Blanchard, Montreal appeared as a French quarter and an English quarter, separated by the buffer zone in which would be found recent immigrants. The 1961 Census showed the same picture and confirmed that the boundary between French- and English-Canada is still along St. Lawrence Blvd, as it was almost a century ago; despite the existence of substantial (but diminishing) English-speaking enclaves in Verdun and St. Ann's Ward, and of a French enclave around the Université de Montréal, it is generally true that the French language predominates in the East, South and North of the Island while English is the universal language of communication in the West and Centre.

Montreal Island is only thirty miles long. All its inhabitants have access to radio and television programs in both languages and there are no serious barriers to prevent mingling of the two major language groups. Despite this, and despite the fact that no test is given by the census enumerator before inscribing a person as bilingual, the 1961 Census reported that there was no section of the island in which even 40% of the citizens claimed to be able to speak both French and English.

As can be seen from the following table, English was spoken by 90% of the population of that part of the island from St. Lawrence Blvd west to Senneville, while only 45% claimed to be able to speak French. In the eastern half of the island, however, the proportions were exactly reversed, with over 90% speaking French and less than 45% speaking English. The northwest and southwest showed crazy-quilt patterns of small areas in which one or the other language was dominant.

Table 53

Percentage of Population claiming ability to speak English and to speak French, specified subdivisions of Montreal Island, 1961 Census

		Percent Speaking		
Sector	*Population*	*Engl. Only*	*Engl. & Fr.*	*French Only*
Westernmost suburbs	85,000	59	28	13
West-Centre	307,000	52	38	8
Northwest	200,000	32	39	24
Southwest	275,000	24	39	38
East	722,000	6	39	53
Easternmost suburbs	157,000	10	32	56

(Figures total less than 100%, due to presence of persons speaking neither of the two languages reported.)

The history of Montreal has been as chequered as is its present population. Founded by Maisonneuve in 1642, the city lived in the shadow of Quebec throughout the French regime (and even, in some respects, for long afterwards: the Université de Montréal remained subject to Laval University until 1920).

After the Capitulation of 1760, English-speaking newcomers took over control of trade and the city grew and prospered. Despite competition from alternative routes through New York State, much of the traffic to and from Upper Canada passed along the St. Lawrence and all the lumber exports of the Ottawa Valley were forwarded through the port of Montreal.

During the period 1830-1865, citizens of British origins were in the majority at Montreal and the Census of 1851 found only 26,020 French-Canadians among a total population of 57,715. However, the extent to which English supremacy was dependent on immigration can be seen from a breakdown of the figure for those of non-French origins: only 12,494 had been born in Canada and the others included 11,736 from Ireland, 3,150 from Scotland and 2,858 from England.

As new areas were opened to settlement in Ontario and as the towns of that province began to rival those of Quebec, the growth of Montreal's English-speaking population slowed appreciably. Between 1851 and 1871, the relative strengths of the two language groups reversed completely; by 1901, almost two-thirds of Montreal's citizens were French-speaking.

Table 54

Population of English, of French and of Other Mother Tongues, Greater Montreal,* Censuses of 1871-1961

<table>
<tr><th></th><th>1871</th><th>1901</th><th>1941</th><th>1951</th><th>1961</th></tr>
<tr><td>French</td><td>87,000</td><td>231,000</td><td>707,000</td><td>906,000</td><td>1,366,000</td></tr>
<tr><td>English</td><td rowspan="2">57,000</td><td rowspan="2">130,000</td><td>295,000</td><td>369,000</td><td>495,000</td></tr>
<tr><td>Other</td><td>115,000</td><td>120,000</td><td>248,000</td></tr>
</table>

*Montreal Island, 1871-1941; metro areas, 1951 & 1961.

The figures show that 65% of Montreal's population gave French as their mother tongue in 1961; this was virtually identical to the 64% reported in 1901. At the turn of the century, however, those of "Other" mother tongues numbered only a few thousand; today, they represent one-third of the non-French community, reflecting the heavy immigration of the postwar years, and their preference for the English language has been an important factor in maintaining the relative strength of the minority group.

Although drawing to itself only a few of the arrivals from overseas, the French-speaking population of Montreal has received heavy reinforcement from the rural areas of Quebec and from Northern New Brunswick (as shown in Table 21 of this book, census figures indicate that there had been a net migration of over 150,000 Canadian-born persons into Montreal during the 1951-1961 decade). Such reinforcement has been necessary, because the birth rate of French Canadians living at Montreal is far below that found in rural parishes and natural increase alone would not have been sufficient to counterbalance immigration.

It is for this reason that the "Back-to-the-Land" movements of the 1930's helped maintain the linguistic status quo at Montreal during a period when immigration from overseas was almost non-existent. The drift of French-Canadians to the metropolis resumed only after 1940, when labor was needed for industries stimulated by wartime demands.

Table 55

Population of Montreal vs. Population of Quebec Province, Persons of French Origin Only, Censuses of 1901-1961

	1901	*1931*	*1941*	*1951*	*1961*
			(thousands of persons)		
Quebec Province	1,321	2,270	2,695	3,327	4,241
Montreal	231	605	699	901	1,353
Montreal/Province	17.5%	26.6%	25.9%	27.0%	31.9%

As in other tables of this chapter, the 1951 and 1961 figures of the above table are for areas which include not only the island of Montreal but, also, Ile Jesus and part of Chambly and other mainland counties, where subuibs such as Longueuil, St. Lambert and Jacques Cartier are now components of the metropolis.

Disregarding the effects of geographical expansion, Montreal's growth during the 1951-1961 decade was due, almost equally, to natural increase (the excess of births over deaths within the metropolis) and to in-migration of persons born elsewhere in Canada or abroad.

As noted in Chapter VII, the movement of population within Canada is no longer broken down by language groups. However, the figures of the following table do indicate the important role that migration, from the other provinces or abroad, has played in the growth of the English-predominant suburbs; as the figures are for the male population of all ages and as a high proportion of the children would be locally-born, it may be inferred that well over half the adult population of these suburbs had been born outside Quebec Province. In sharp contrast, a very high proportion of the citizens of the French-predominant suburbs were Quebec-born.

Table 56

Places of Birth of Male Populations, Six English-predominant vs. Eight French-predominant Suburbs of Montreal, 1961 Census

Place of Birth	*6 English-predominant suburbs**	*8 French-predominant suburbs***
Quebec Province	60%	90%
Ontario	10	2
Atlantic Provinces	4	1½
Western Provinces	4	½
United Kingdom	9	1
United States	3	½
Other Countries	10	4½

*Beaconsfield, Cote St. Luke, Dorval, Pointe Claire, Town of Mount Royal and Westmount; of the total population, only 19% gave their mother tongue as French.

**Duvernay, Jacques Cartier, Laval des Rapides, Montreal North, Pointe aux Trembles, Pont Viau, R. des Prairies and St. Vincent de Paul; 87% French mother tongue.

In comparing the characteristics of the two groups of suburbs, it is quite remarkable that the average income of heads of families in the English suburbs was almost exactly double that found in the French suburbs. An even greater disparity was found when the number of those who had attended university was expressed as a percentage of the total population.

This superiority in education and in earning power has given the English-speaking community a degree of influence much greater than its mere numbers would command, to such an extent that English is still the dominant language in industry and commerce.

Table 57

Number of Adult Males speaking English and speaking French, Montreal, 1961 Census

	As Mother Tongue	*As Minor Language*	*Proportion Speaking*
French	387,484	106,340	78.6%
English	142,017	355,284	79.2%
Others	98,740	—	—

The above figures are for the adult males, that part of the population which must go out every day and mingle with others. Among the women of Montreal, there is not the same degree of bilingualism; this, and the fact that in the stores it is the language of the customer which prevails, has made French the dominant language in retailing and has given the downtown shopping areas an increasingly French aspect in recent years.

Although the two language groups may meet during their working hours, Table 53 has shown that each tends to retire to its own sections of town when evening falls. A closer examination of the two communities suggests that it is not only language that divides them; in many ways, this is the least of their differences, or so it would appear at many bilingual meetings.

The French are, generally, tightly bound to their community. They usually belong to Catholic parishes and their families have been living (and intermarrying) in Quebec Province for three centuries. Thanks to a quite distinctive system of education, their "élite" are, typically, priests or lawyers or doctors; consequently, they predominate chiefly in the Church and in Government.

In sharp contrast, the English-speaking citizens (including the high proportion of immigrants who have assimilated to the English language)

predominate in industry, finance and commerce. However, they have no real common denominator except language, being of all religions, ethnic origins and places of birth.

The 1961 Census found that slightly fewer than half were Protestant, one in eight being of the Jewish faith and three in eight belonging to the Catholic Church. Almost half the adults had been born outside Canada; of the Canadian-born, many had passed their early years in other provinces.

In chapter XV, we suggested that any coercive measures taken against the use of the English language in Quebec could result in departure of those who prefer to work in that language. Such a reaction could have particularly serious effects on the future of Montreal.

It is true that some members of the English-speaking community are in occupations which are of only marginal benefit to the province and their departure, for Ontario or elsewhere, would not be of too much importance. However, Quebec can certainly not afford any mass exodus of the professional and managerial personnel who are now working in Montreal and aiding the province's tax revenues as well as keeping the wheels of industry turning.

It seems probable, therefore, that English will be allowed to remain a language of work in the metropolis for many decades to come, although not to the exclusion of French, and that there will be no curtailment of the schools and other facilities now enjoyed by the minority.

If this is so, if there is to be no actual harassment of the non-French population by government or by others, then what may be Montreal's linguistic future?

As noted in Chapter XIV, about 95,000 persons of French mother tongue are now reaching their majority annually in Quebec Province and the figure will rise to 110,000 by 1981. Tables 43 and 21 show the extent to which Montreal has, in the past, received the excess population of the rural areas; with labor needs diminishing in agriculture and the forest industries, this movement off the land will accelerate.

It seems probable, therefore, that the number of French-Canadians moving into Montreal each year will increase, perhaps quite substantially; not until 1985, at the very earliest, will the present decline in Quebec birth rates have any effect on this movement.

The volume and nature of future immigration is impossible to predict but it does seem likely that an increasing proportion of the immigrants settling at Montreal will assimilate to the French language and that those who wish their children to learn English will continue on to Ontario. Meanwhile, inter-provincial migration could well result in a considerable net outflow of English-speaking Montrealers, for the reasons given in Chapter XV.

On balance, therefore, it appears most likely that the relative strength of the English language at Montreal will continue to decline. However, under present conditions, there appears to be very little likelihood of a mass exodus of English-speakers, such as was observed at Quebec City a century ago.

CHAPTER XVIII

Canada's Capital

The previous chapter described a city in which the English-speaking minority is becoming increasingly uneasy at the prospect that, after two centuries of almost unchallenged primacy, their language may soon cease to be the one guaranteeing advancement. In Ottawa, however, English appears to be solidly established as the language of work and it is only within the past few years that any serious proposals have been made that French-Canadians be allowed to use their own language during office hours.

Despite this handicap under which they must work, the French-speaking minority at Ottawa has one very real advantage not possessed by the English-speaking minority at Montreal. No matter how far west the latter may move on their island, they are still within the boundaries of Quebec Province and subject to laws made by French-Canadian legislators for the benefit of a predominantly-French-Canadian electorate.

The minority working in Ottawa, however, may return each evening to residential suburbs located within La Belle Province, where their own language group dominates all levels of government. Their children attend schools in which the language of instruction is French and their wives have radio, television and shopping facilities available in their own language. Housing on this side of the river is often designed with the needs and budgets of the average French-Canadian family in view, but more expensive tastes can be satisfied in such new developments as Parc de la Montagne.

There is, too, a predominance of the French language in rural areas north and east of the capital, giving the minority group a solid hinterland, so all factors combine to produce a linguistic segregation that is even more noticeable at Ottawa than at Montreal.

Just over half the population of French mother tongue were living on the Quebec side of the river in 1961 and, of those in Ontario, the majority were in that part of Ottawa (including Eastview) which lies east of the Rideau Canal and north of the Queensway; a glance at the map shows that these areas are contiguous, communicating across the Interprovincial

Bridge, and form a geographical entity in the northern part of the capital area.

In Hull County, 89 % of the population is of French mother tongue and those who speak "French Only" are more numerous than those who speak "French and English"; the other extreme is found in the southwestern part of Ottawa, where barely one person in eight could speak French as even a second or third language.

Table 58

Number of Persons claiming ability to speak English and to speak French, specified subdivisions of the Ottawa/Hull area, 1961 Census

	French Only	*English & French*	*English Only*
Hull	39,500	37,900	5,000
Lucerne, Aylmer, Deschênes	2,400	6,400	5,300
Eastview & N. E. Ottawa	9,000	41,200	33,300
North-central Ottawa	1,500	15,200	38,000
Rockcliffe, eastern Ottawa & Gloucester	3,600	17,200	53,600
S. W. Ottawa & Nepean	800	14,600	101,000
Metropolitan area	56,700	132,500	236,300

These census figures confirm the general impression that the English-speaking residents of Ottawa seldom learn the language of their neighbors. This is due, at least in part, to the economic dominance of the English language: although the 1961 Census reported the average income of a family head in Ottawa as $5,165, the breakdown by sectors showed averages of only $3,600 in Lower Town, $3,894 in Hull and $4,121 in Eastview, the areas where those who speak French are in the majority.

The history of Ottawa shows that the capital area, like the Valley as a whole, was completely neglected during the French regime, the first settlers being New Englanders, followed by Irish immigrants. The French-Canadians were latecomers and their arrival was hardly welcomed by the Irish whom they displaced in the logging shanties and sawmills; even today, some of this old animosity remains.

By 1871, persons of French origin made up just over one-third the population of Ottawa and about half that of Hull. Until Confederation, the two sides of the Ottawa River had developed without regard for political boundaries and it is interesting to note that Argenteuil County, in Quebec, was still two-thirds British-origin while Prescott County, in Ontario, reported a French-origin majority.

Once Ottawa had been chosen as capital of the new dominion, its character began to change as white-collar jobs in the new civil service attracted recruits from all over Canada. The French-speaking element of the city's population reached a peak of relative strength in 1881 and has been declining since, while such industrial suburbs as Hull and Gatineau were becoming increasingly French.

During the postwar years, a new factor accentuated the linguistic segregation as the capital area experienced the flight to suburbia common to all North American cities.

Each language group tended to move outward from its own sections of the city. For the English-speaking families, this usually meant the purchase of a house in one of the many new developments south and west of the old city, within areas which were, subsequently, annexed to Ottawa.

The predominantly-French section of Ottawa, however, was in the north end of the city, jammed up against the Ottawa River; the interprovincial boundary prevented the city from expanding its limits in this direction, so the younger French-Canadians have had to leave the city.

The extent to which there has been an actual exodus of the family-forming group is indicated by the age distribution of those of French mother tongue remaining within the City of Ottawa: in 1961, those in the 0-9 age group were hardly more numerous than those who had passed their 54th birthday. Of the 40,000 children of French mother tongue in the capital area, almost 23,000 were on the Quebec side of the river, about 6,500 were in Eastview and Gloucester, and only 10,500 could be found within the City of Ottawa.

This exodus has, of course, caused the relative strength of Ottawa's French-speaking population to drop sharply, accelerating the trend that had been evident since the beginning of this century.

Table 59

Population of French Mother Tongue vs. Total Population, City of Ottawa, Censuses of 1871-1961

	1871	*1901*	*1921*	*1941*	*1961*
Total population	21,500	57,600	108,000	155,000	268,000
of French M.T.*	7,200	19,000	30,400	44,600	56,900
French/Total	33%	33%	28%	29%	21%

* "Ethnic Origin French" in 1871, 1901 and 1921.

Reflecting this drop in the importance of the French-speaking electorate, no mayor of French mother tongue has been elected since 1948. As a gesture of friendship toward the minority group, the last redistribution of the city's wards was made in such a way as to leave two (of the ten) with French-speaking majorities, ensuring continued representation of this group on City Council; had it not been for this little gerrymander (it required only 4,200 votes to elect the average French-speaking alderman in 1964, as against 5,600 for those representing non-French wards), the influence of the French-speaking citizens in the affairs of Ottawa would have vanished almost completely.

In contrast to the decline of the French language at Ottawa, the Catholic religion has increased its relative strength as some 11,500 postwar immigrants joined the always-strong native-born Catholic population. This, however, has merely compounded the misery of the French-speaking group, since they are now in the minority among even those of their own religion.

Table 60

Population of French Mother Tongue vs. Population professing Catholic Religion, Censuses of 1911-1961

	1911	*1941*	*1951*	*1961*
R. Catholics	43,245	76,607	95,468	128,197
of French M.T.*	26,732	44,638	50,290	56,882
Ratio	62%	58%	53%	44%

*Including a few non-Catholics.

At the time of the bitterest disputes for control of the Separate School treasury, in 1913-1916, Catholics of French origin held a two-to-one majority over those of all other origins combined. At present, each language group has approximately equal strength among those voting in Separate School elections and an informal, but strictly observed, agreement provides that each should elect five of the ten Board members. It will be a bitter blow to the French if, as seems likely, the present trend continues and they drop to a minority position on even the School Board that they have effectively dominated for the past century.

At present, the future of the French language within the City of Ottawa is so unpromising that several politicians have recommended that a federal district be formed, to throw into the scales such overwhelmingly-French areas as Hull and Eastview. The population of the metropolitan area under discussion would show a more nearly equal balance of the two major language groups; according to proponents of the scheme, this would better protect those of the French-language group than does the present system of independent municipalities, each favoring its own majority.

Table 61

Population of French Mother Tongue vs. Total Population, National Capital Area, Censuses of 1901-1961

	1901	*1941*	*1951*	*1961*
Total population	80,000	215,000	282,000	430,000
of French M.T.	35,000	87,000	115,000	162,000
French/Total	44%	40%	41%	38%

Although formation of a federal district might be of some benefit to the 57,000 French-Canadians living within the City of Ottawa, the scheme might well work to the overall detriment of the French language; not only would it result in loss of independence for such suburbs as Eastview, where the French-speaking group is so solidly in control that no non-French alderman has ever been elected, but it might, also, strike a mortal blow at the hopes of survival of the minority elsewhere in Ontario.

Ottawa is the focal point of all French-language activities in this province. In the square mile east of the Rideau Canal will be found the three pillars of Franco-Ontarian prestige: their archbishop, their university and their newspaper. In the same area will be found "La Maison franco-ontarienne" and the headquarters of most of the organizations responsible for preservation of the French language in Ontario; remove Ottawa, and the remaining French-speaking population of Ontario would be an incoherent, semi-rural minority without natural leaders or a central rallying point.

The future of the French language at Ottawa is, therefore, of major significance; as Ottawa goes, so, too, could go the entire area west of the interprovincial boundary.

CHAPTER XIX

Ontario

Although French outposts had flourished on Georgian Bay during the first half of the 17th Century (the recently-restored Ste. Marie has become a major tourist attraction), these were shortlived and the only real settlement in Ontario at the end of the French Regime was that which had been founded at Detroit in 1701.

Until well into the 19th Century, the French inhabitants of the Essex Peninsula, the descendants of the Detroit settlers, continued to be the only important group of that language in Upper Canada. For their benefit, French was permitted as a language of instruction in the local schools, just as German was permitted in the Kitchener area. In 1887, the prestige of this little community reached its peak, when Dr. C. E. Casgrain was appointed to be the first French-Canadian senator from outside Quebec.

However, the Peninsula was very remote from other French-speaking areas and subjected to strong anglicizing influences from the United States as well as from the surrounding areas of its own province. Despite the desperate resistance of a few ardent "nationalists", it soon became evident that English would be the universal language of Southern Ontario.

In August, 1910, therefore, the newly-appointed Bishop of London, Michael Fallon, made a statement of policy to his diocesan clergy, in which he denounced the slogan, "La Langue, gardienne de la Foi", as being a creation of French-speaking politicians and not of the Church. He went on to state his conviction that "bilingual" schools were, by their very nature, unable to give the type of education that was required in Southern Ontario, and that they should be discontinued.

Today, half a century later, there are still some French-Canadians at Windsor but the community is ageing and its disappearance may well be imminent. Although the 1961 Census reported 5,819 children of French ethnic origin, in Metropolitan Windsor, it could find only 990 of the same age group who were of French mother tongue; the inference is that 83% of the younger generation has already been assimilated.

The following table shows that, for the Peninsula as a whole (including rural areas), those who speak French are declining in actual number, not merely in relative strength.

Table 62

Population of French Mother Tongue vs. Total Population, Essex and Kent Counties, Censuses of 1871-1961

	1871	*1901*	*1941*	*1951*	*1961*
Total Population	60,000	91,000	241,000	296,000	348,000
of French M.T.	14,000	22,000	35,000	35,000	32,000
French/Total	24%	24%	14%	12%	9%

Elsewhere in Southern Ontario, the 1961 Census found only 86,000 persons of French mother tongue. Most of these are dispersed to such an extent that they lack the parish and other organizations essential for even the barest survival; the consequence is that assimilation appears inevitable.

Welland is the notable exception to the above generalization: some 6,000 French-Canadians represent 17% of the city's population and have, so far, retained their language reasonably well. However, this little colony was established only in 1917, when workers had to be brought in from Quebec during a wartime labor shortage, so assimilation has not yet had time to make any serious inroads.

In the metropolitan area of Toronto, there were 26,000 persons of French mother tongue (including 3,300 born outside Canada) but they represented only 1.4% of the total population; in this area, Italian, German, Ukrainian, Polish and Yiddish (in that order) outranked French among the mother tongues. The situation was similar at Hamilton, Kitchener and London; among the 40,000 children of school age in that last city, only 150 reported French as their first language.

Examining the census figures for the youngest age groups, it would appear that about 80% of those of French origin living in Southern Ontario have adopted English as the language of the home. Since many of those who still retain the French language are quite recent arrivals from Quebec or New Brunswick, it would seem that assimilation has been almost complete among those brought up in the area, except at Welland and in the rural parishes around Windsor.

Such massive assimilation is not too surprising when it is considered that those who claim to be able to speak French, including the many for whom it is only a second or third language, make up only 4½% of the total population of Southern Ontario; anyone who speaks only French is under a heavy handicap, both economically and socially, and, from bilingualism, it is only one more step to assimilation. The trend is accelerated by the fact that there are very few segregated parishes, so the incidence of linguistically-mixed marriages is quite high, with the children usually being brought up in English.

Although the industrial cities of Southern Ontario do attract a steady stream of new French-speakers from Quebec and New Brunswick, the numbers involved do not appear to be great and even this small flow of reinforcements will, probably, dry up as Quebec increases its own employment capacity. Barring some totally unexpected change in the environment, the future of the French language in this region is not promising.

In sharp contrast to this rather gloomy picture of the French-speaking population of Southern Ontario, the minority living in the northern counties has survived reasonably well and that of Eastern Ontario could, almost, be described as flourishing. The following table shows the figures for the eleven counties which stretch from Cornwall to Sault Ste. Marie, across the top of Ontario, and contrasts these with the corresponding figures for the rest of the province.

Table 63

Population of French Mother Tongue, Northern and Eastern Ontario vs. Southern and Western Ontario, Censuses of 1871-1961

	1871	*1901*	*1941*	*1951*	*1961*
North and East	32,000	94,000	218,000	247,000	307,000
Elsewhere	43,000	64,000	71,000	94,000	118,000

During the ninety years covered by the above table, the total population of Southern Ontario increased from 1,467,000 to 5,174,000 while that of the North and East increased from 153,000 to 1,062,000. Relative to the total population, therefore, the French of the border counties increased their importance, from 21% to 29%, while those of the interior were declining from 3% to 2%.

Movement of French-Canadians into Eastern Ontario had begun early in the 19th Century, when settlers from Vaudreuil and the Montreal area entered Prescott County through L'Orignal; as a seigneurie, this had not been homesteaded by the earlier waves of British-origin settlers. By 1871, the new arrivals were in the majority in Prescott County; by 1901, they were the major element in Russell County and dominated the entire Lower Ottawa.

The political boundary between Quebec and Ontario has not been revised since 1791 and still follows the ethno-linguistic frontier as it existed at that date. The ecclesiastical authorities, however, have been more responsive to demographic changes and, in 1847, the parishes of the Ottawa Valley were detached from the Diocese of Kingston and entrusted to an Oblate who had arrived from France only a few years earlier.

Under Bishop Guigues and his successor, Archbishop Duhamel (1874-1910), the tens of thousands of French-Canadians who poured into Eastern and Northern Ontario were assured of parishes and schools in which their own language would have priority. In 1910, the Archdiocese of Ottawa became a haven to which embattled Franco-Ontarian groups could retire after the bishops of Southern Ontario had come out publicly in favor of assimilation of all minorities to the English language.

At present, French is the most important language in that part of Ontario lying east of Cornwall and, except in that city, assimilation has been negligible; English is of so little importance that over half the French-Canadians living in Prescott and Russell Counties reported to the 1961 Census that they spoke "French Only".

Table 64

Population of British, of French and of Other Origins in Prescott, Russell,* Glengarry and Stormont Counties, Censuses of 1871-1961

Origin:	*1871*	*1901*	*1931*	*1951*	*1961*
French	18,800	47,400	56,400	69,300	76,800
British	41,900	46,700	32,800	34,000	37,400
Others	5,100	7,200	5,000	6,000	11,000

*Russell County adjusted to 1961 boundaries for all years.

It is interesting to note, in this area, the same phenomenon already observed in the Eastern Townships and other regions of Quebec Province: an actual departure of the British-origin population, who abandoned their lands to the incoming French. Of the British-origin population within the four counties in 1961, almost half were living in the city of Cornwall (it might be noted in passing that, contrary to what appears to be a common belief, only 42% of the population of that city were of French mother tongue in 1961).

For the average resident of Eastern Ontario, there is no difficulty in retaining the French language. Television and radio stations at Montreal and Ottawa blanket the area, newspapers are available from both cities and there has never been a lack of contact with the French-speaking heartland. Elected representatives at all levels are usually French-Canadians and their control of the local separate school boards assures the use of their language in the classrooms; under the Bishop of Alexandria and the Archbishop of Ottawa, both French-Canadians, adequate French-language parishes are assured. To the extent, therefore, that they are willing to remain in their economically-depressed region, the French-Canadians of Eastern Ontario should be secure from assimilation.

In Northern Ontario, however, forces are at work which have begun to make inroads among the younger generation and assimilation is on the increase. The substantial mining industry of the northern counties has drawn many non-French to the region and these have always outnumbered the "colons" who came up the Ottawa from Montreal after the Clay Belt had been made accessible by completion of the C.P.R., in 1885.

Table 65

Population of French Mother Tongue vs. Total Population, Cochrane, Nipissing, Sudbury and Timiskaming Counties, Censuses of 1911-1961

	1911	*1941*	*1951*	*1961*
Total Population	74,000	255,000	294,000	383,000
of French M.T.	26,000	93,000	110,000	138,000
French/Total	35%	36%	38%	36%

An ever-increasing contact with the English-speaking majority has led to 28% assimilation among the younger French ethnics in Nipissing County and Sudbury County; Timiskaming is not far behind, with 23%, while the rate was only 13% in Cochrane County. Had it not been for this assimilation, the percentage of French in the four counties would have increased, rather than decreased, between 1951 and 1961.

Some figures for the eleven counties of the north and east illustrate the importance of assimilation in keeping down the relative importance of the French-speaking population in even such areas as are in constant contact with Quebec. In reading this table, it should be kept in mind that even some of those who give their mother tongue as French no longer use that language in the home.

Table 66

Population of French Origin and Population of French Mother Tongue vs. Total Population, Eleven Counties of Northern and Eastern Ontario, Censuses of 1941-1961

	1941	*1951*	*1961*
Total Population	667,000	777,000	1,062,000
of French Origin	238,000 (36%)	284,000 (37%)	366,000 (34%)
of French M.T.	218,000 (33%)	247,000 (32%)	307,000 (29%)

The 1961 Census figures given above were for the population of all ages and show that persons "of French Mother Tongue" were 16% less numerous than those "of French Origin". Among the youngest age group, the difference was 27%; this indicates that assimilation is on the increase in the border counties, although not yet even remotely comparable to that which we have found in Southern Ontario.

Summing up the situation in Ontario, the French language has very little likelihood of survival in the southern parts of the province, except as a second language among those who will find it of economic or cultural value. In Eastern Ontario, its prospects are reasonably bright and in the north it should have at least a fighting chance as provincial subsidies and other encouragement revivify the "bilingual" schools. However, the odds are heavy: no longer is it possible for French-speaking communities to live in isolation and the younger generation is increasingly exposed to intermarriage and economic enticement, the two major roads to assimilation.

CHAPTER XX

The West

The early history of the Prairie Provinces was of fur-traders, those of English origin entering through Hudson's Bay and those of French origin up the Great Lakes system from Montreal. Both groups were interested only in trading and no serious attempt at colonization was made while the territory remained under the jurisdiction of the Hudson's Bay Company, the one exception being that of Lord Selkirk.

However, the United States was expanding westward and Minnesota had a substantial population by the mid-19th Century. Climate studies showed that the region north of the 49th parallel was suitable for agriculture and it became obvious that the Imperial Government had only two choices: colonize the Prairies under British rule or allow them to fall into the possession of the United States, as Oregon had done in 1846.

Confederation opened the way for annexation of the West to Canada, including not only the Prairies but, also, the crown colony on the Pacific. The latter had, of course, a history of its own, mineral wealth having attracted to it many thousands of prospectors and giving it a character entirely different from that of the Prairies.

Even before 1870, a westward movement had begun from Ontario and the pace of this accelerated after Wolseley's expedition. Meanwhile, Archbishop Taché had been sending emissaries to the overpopulated parishes of Quebec in an attempt to recruit French-speaking colonists.

The failure of the latter has already been mentioned in chapter XI; Table 67, on the next page, shows that westward migration from Ontario outpaced that from Quebec by a margin of six-to-one.

In 1931, after which westward migration virtually ceased, there were 152,000 persons of French ethnic origin living west of the Great Lakes. Of these, 96,000 had been born in the West, 8,000 were immigrants from France and fewer than 48,000 had come from Eastern Canada. At that date, there were 371,000 French-Canadian immigrants living in the United States; eight times as many had gone south as had gone to the Canadian West.

Table 67

Provinces of Birth of Persons living in the Western Provinces, Censuses of 1881-1921

	1881	*1891*	*1901*	*1911*	*1921*
Ontario	20,800	71,900	121,500	273,000	292,000
Quebec	4,600	12,000	18,300	41,900	53,000
Maritimes	2,100	8,800	14,800	39,600	47,900

This indifference on the part of French-Canadians toward westward migration had a two-fold consequence. The more important was that the social matrix of the Prairie Provinces was formed by the Anglo-Protestants from Ontario; immigrants from Central and Eastern Europe assimilated almost entirely to the English language.

Also important, however, was the fact that the few French-Canadians who had gone west soon found themselves hopelessly outnumbered and saw their children exposed to assimilative forces that became particularly strong after 1931 when the old rural isolation began to break up. As a consequence, the number of persons in the Western Provinces who speak French has been increasing only slowly in recent decades, assimilation eating away most of the natural increase.

Table 68

Population of French Mother Tongue vs. Total Population, Four Western Provinces, Censuses of 1901-1961

	1901	*1931*	*1961*
Total Population	646,000	3,062,000	4,846,000
M.T. French	30,000	121,000	167,000
French/Total	4.6%	4.0%	3.4%

The drift away from the farm has affected French-Canadians as much as those of other origins and 40% of those of French mother tongue now live in major cities. Here, they are almost lost among the English-speaking citizens: at Edmonton, there are only 11,200 French among a total population of 338,000 and at Vancouver (total population 790,000) the 13,300 French-Canadians are less numerous than the 15,200 persons who gave Chinese as their mother tongue. Not surprisingly, assimilation has been particularly high in these metropolitan centres.

In addition to the movement from rural into urban areas, there has been some interprovincial movement, with Alberta and British Columbia gaining population at the expense of Saskatchewan. Because it separates the young adults from the French-language parishes of their childhood, this movement, too, has weakened the resistance to assimilation.

Table 69

Population of French Mother Tongue in Each of the Western Provinces, Censuses of 1901-1961

	1901	*1931*	*1941*	*1951*	*1961*
Manitoba	16,000	42,500	51,500	54,200	60,900
Saskatchewan	7,000 (Saskatchewan and Alberta combined)	42,300	43,700	36,800	36,200
Alberta		28,100	31,500	34,200	42,300
B.C.	4,600	7,800	11,100	19,400	26,200

The above figures are for the French-speaking population of all ages. Referring back to Table 15, it will be noticed that there were 28,600 children (aged 0-9) of French mother tongue in the West in 1931, virtually the same total (28,800) as found by the 1961 Census. In other words, the number of French-speaking children has not increased during a 30-year period in which the number of non-French children has almost doubled (to 1,100,000 in 1961).

On the average, each French-speaking child is now surrounded by 38 English-speaking children; assimilation appears inevitable under such circumstances.

The Catholic Church recognized the ascendancy of the English language in the West over half a century ago. It was in September of 1910 that Archbishop Bourne announced to the hierarchy of Canada that the policy of Rome would, thenceforward, be to appoint English-speaking bishops in the Western Provinces. Despite vigorous protests from Quebec, words were followed by action: a new archdiocese, that of Winnipeg, was erected in 1915 to serve the Catholics of Manitoba and the Archbishop of St. Boniface was left with only his title and the predominantly-French southeast corner of the province. Calgary had been entrusted to a bishop of Irish origin in 1913 and Regina had followed shortly after; within a decade of the speech at Montreal, French-speaking bishops could be found only in odd corners where they would exercise only limited influence toward preservation of the French language in the West.

Although the disappearance of their language appears inevitable, the French-speaking population of the West (or, more precisely, those who claim to speak for them) are far from resigned to this fate. Like a mortally-wounded animal, their last fight may be more vigorous than any previous, and just as hopeless.

Manitoba:

La Verendrye had explored what is now Manitoba during the period 1731-1743 and there was a constant flow of trappers and missionaries into the West during the succeeding century, but the little settlement on the Red River had a white population of only 1,600 in 1871. Fort Garry was described as being: "A little camp with a wall around it to keep the Indians back" and St. Boniface was the most important centre on the Prairies, the seat of an archbishop with jurisdiction over all Catholics in the vast area stretching from the Great Lakes to the Pacific Coast.

Sections 22 and 23 of the Act whereby Manitoba became part of Canada in 1870 had provided for equality of the French and English languages and for continuation of denominational schools, presumably on the assumption that Archbishop Taché's recruiting efforts would meet with at least some success. This, however, did not occur and both sections were, effectively, revoked by the provincial legislature in 1890.

Official connivance has, actually, permitted use of French in the schools of areas where the population is predominantly French-speaking; elsewhere, there are private schools and a report published in 1961 stated that some 10,000 pupils were then receiving French-language instruction in 130 schools, and that there were 400 studying at the collège classique in St. Boniface. However, the trend toward larger schools is being felt, as French-controlled local boards disappear through amalgamation and as the cost of distinct schools continues to rise.

French-language radio (CKSB, since 1946) and even television (CBWFT, since 1960) can be received by the majority of Franco-Manitobans and the provincial legislature appears to be taking at least some first steps toward giving financial assistance to French-language schools, but the milieu is not favorable to survival of the minority language. In the province as a whole, barely one person in twelve claimed to be able to speak French, including those for whom it was only a second or third tongue; even in St. Boniface, 60% of the citizens stated that they spoke "English Only".

The Franco-Manitobans have resisted assimilation more effectively than have the minorities in the other Western Provinces, but the 1961 Census reported only 6,341 children of French mother tongue, as against 12,337 of French origin (aged 0 to 4, in each case). This could well indicate that the actual numbers, and not merely the relative strength, of those who retain the old language will soon start to fall.

Saskatchewan:

After settlers from Ontario had begun to arrive in large numbers in Manitoba, many of the French-speaking Métis moved further west, into northern Saskatchewan. Their subsequent support of Riel did not help the public image of French-Canadians in general and the use of their language was abolished in the legislature and most of the schools by acts of the Territorial Assembly passed in 1892.

Today, those of French mother tongue make up less than 4% of the population of Saskatchewan, their number having actually declined from 44,000 in 1941 to 36,000 in 1961 while the total population of the province was increasing from 896,000 to 925,000; this decline is largely attributable to assimilation, which has affected two-thirds of the younger generation.

Almost half the French-speaking population of Saskatchewan will be found in a band stretching across the northern part of the province and is under the spiritual authority of a French-speaking bishop resident in the City of Prince Albert. The great dispersion of this group has left it quite vulnerable to assimilation.

In sharp contrast is the French colony centred on Gravelbourg. Numbering hardly more than 5,000, this community is tightly-knit and has not only a bishop but, also, a radio station (CFRG, since 1952) and a collège classique affiliated with the University of Ottawa; although resistance to assimilation has been high in this area, its population is so small that its influence is limited.

Saskatoon has had a French-language radio station since 1952, but that city's population of 96,000 includes only 1,764 persons of French mother tongue. At Regina, the proportion is similar, 1,897 among 112,000, and, in both cities, the 1961 Census indicated that five out of six of the younger generation of French origin are now using English as the language of the home.

Of the three Prairie Provinces, Saskatchewan would appear to be the one in which the French tongue is weakest.

Alberta:

Small settlements of French-speaking Métis were reported in the vicinity of what is now Edmonton as far back as 1814 and "La Mission Ste-Anne" was founded in this area in 1842; by 1871, the Catholic (chiefly French-speaking) population of the region was sufficiently important that an episcopal see was erected at St. Albert.

Between 1901 and 1931, the French-speaking population of Alberta increased ten-fold, keeping pace with the population as a whole. In recent years, however, the effects of assimilation have become increasingly apparent: as a proportion of the total population of the province, those of French mother tongue declined from 3.8% in 1931 to 3.2% in 1961; an even more rapid decline in future decades is indicated by the fact that only 2.2% of the children of school age gave their mother tongue as French.

Table 12 has shown that assimilation reached 80%, in 1961, among persons of French origin living in the cities of Alberta, as against 42% among those who had remained on the land. However, the trend away from the farm is irreversible and fewer than half the Franco-Albertans remain in the rural parishes under the jurisdiction of French-speaking bishops, so the overall rate of assimilation can be expected to accelerate. This, despite the fact that school laws permit the early years to be given in French, with teachers supplied from a French-language normal school opened at Edmonton in 1963.

Three-quarters of the French-speaking residents of Alberta are to be found in the northern parts of the province: 7,500 in the Diocese of Grouard (the Peace River country), 9,000 in the Diocese of St. Paul (the north-east) and 15,000 in the vicinity of Edmonton. There are only 4,000 at Calgary, among a total population of 318,000, and the remaining 5,000 are scattered among the 434,000 persons living in the other ten census divisions.

British Columbia:

Although Spanish, British and Russian sea captains were frequent visitors to the Pacific Coast of what is now Canada, French names are conspicuously absent from the early history of this province. A priest from Quebec, Father Demers, arrived on the coast in 1839 and was appointed Bishop of Vancouver in 1847 but distance discouraged any sizable migration of French-Canadians.

One movement of note, however, was that arranged in 1909 by the Fraser Mills Lumber Company, which recruited workers in the Ottawa-Hull region. With these men came their families and also an Oblate priest, Father Maillard; a self-contained town with church and school was set up three miles from New Westminster. Today, the 600 French-speaking families in Maillardville form the most important community of that language west of the Rockies.

As recently as 1931, there were only 15,082 persons of French ethnic origin in the entire province and half of these had been assimilated. Wartime and postwar immigration from the Prairie Provinces and the East, although of some importance, usually involved only individuals or small groups and these have tended to assimilate rapidly, the process being accelerated by the fact that marriages between French-Canadians have been only a fraction of those involving linguistically-mixed partners.

The 1961 Census reported that, in a population of 1,629,000, only 60,000 claimed to be able to speak French, including almost 34,000 for whom it was merely a second or third tongue. There were only three French-language parishes in the province and "bilingual" schools receive no tax support; the entire milieu, without French-language newspapers, radio or television, is strongly anglicizing.

Generally, the weakness of the French language in British Columbia is second only to that found at the other extremity of the country, in Newfoundland.

CHAPTER XXI

Maîtres Chez Nous

Two voices appear to be crying out simultaneously from Quebec. One demands equality of opportunity for French-Canadians from coast to coast, while the other proclaims the doctrine of "Maîtres chez nous".

To understand this paradox, it is necessary to review the history of the French-speaking population of North America. This can be divided into four distinct phases, the first three being: the initial period of expansion into Louisiana and Western Canada, the catastrophes of 1755-1765 and the subsequent period of expansion that continued until the end of the 19th Century.

Not all French-Canadians have had the courage to read their history books past this point. To those who are aware of the fourth phase, the bitter disappointments of the 20th Century and the withdrawal into the Soo-Moncton limits, the first group are mere dreamers; to quote Professor Brunet: "Il faut constater, une fois de plus, le poids de l'héritage pernicieux d'un certain messianisme. Il se trouve encore en 1963 des Canadiens français pour rêver du jour où on parlera français à Toronto, Halifax et Vancouver comme on parle anglais à Montréal".*

To the realists, the other provinces have been lost. Let those who wish to speak French (and to have their grandchildren speak French) concentrate on the development of their language within the one political entity ("état") in which they have complete control of the government. This is not separatism, in the political sense; it is the doctrine of "Maîtres chez nous".

French Canadians have had more than their share of disappointments in the past. Under the French crown, the colony was never sent enough soldiers or enough settlers and a census taken in 1765, after repatriation to France of those who did not wish to live under English rule, showed a total population of only 80,000: not quite 70,000 along the St. Lawrence, 10,000 in the Maritimes and perhaps 1,000 in such scattered outposts as Detroit and Michilimackinac.

*Michel Brunet, quoted in Le Devoir of December 17, 1963.

As a consequence, the Eastern Townships, the Gaspé Peninsula, the Ottawa Valley and the Laurentian Foothills were still virgin territory in 1765, and were soon occupied by English-speaking settlers and lumbermen. During the early decades of the 19th Century, Loyalists and New Englanders, later reinforced by immigrants from Britain and Ireland, formed a ring around the French counties while English-speaking citizens were in the majority at Montreal and constituted a very strong minority at Quebec City.

The third phase, however, had already begun. Driven by the population pressures that were building up within the older parishes, the young men and women of French Canada began to push steadily outward into all the periphery of Quebec Province and across the Ottawa River into Eastern Ontario.

By 1851, there were 700,000 French-Canadians and their outward progress was, to an ever-increasing extent, bringing them into counties already populated by those of British origin. However, the latter were, at just this time, being attracted away by the new lands being opened to farming in Ontario and the West, so conflict between the two language groups was kept to a minimum.

The first census after Confederation showed that those of French origin were in the majority in all except a few areas of Quebec Province; 1871 was also the first year in which French-speaking citizens were in the majority at Montreal.

Counting Acadians and the Métis of the West, there were some 1,100,000 French-speaking persons in Canada in 1871 and a folk-myth began to grow: the French-Canadians would become sufficiently numerous to dominate the country, because God had willed for them a messianic mission (to quote a quite recent book by a professor of l'Université de Sherbrooke: "Dieu avait besoin d'un peuple français et catholique en Amérique").

Even the more serious French-Canadian historians write of the period 1851-1901 as if they were describing the campaigns of a successful conqueror. The names of counties and the dates at which their French-speaking inhabitants became the majority are recited as would be a list of victories: Wolfe and Shefford in 1861, Drummond and Prescott (Ontario) in 1871, Richmond, Sherbrooke, Compton and Russell (Ontario) by 1901. At the end of the century, only five counties in Quebec Province still showed English-speaking majorities and both New Brunswick and Ontario appeared ripe for conquest.

The turn of the century, however, marked the beginning of the fourth phase. Almost imperceptibly, the massive emigration towards New England had drained the vitality of French Canada. During the final decades of the 19th Century, the Prairie Provinces had received six times as many settlers from Ontario as from Quebec and were irretrievably lost to the French language when the immigrants from Central and Eastern Europe assimilated to the majority they found established in their new homeland.

Hopelessly outnumbered, left virtually without reinforcements and, usually, with only very limited financial resources, the French-Canadians of the Western Provinces, like those of Southern Ontario, were capable only of withdrawing into little enclaves while their children inexorably assimilated to the language of the surrounding multitudes.

Closer to Quebec, the Franco-Ontarians of the eastern and northern counties were able to retain their language and even to pass it down to the present generation. However, theirs was an operation of mere survival and they did not have the numbers or the resources to seriously aid their cousins in the South of Ontario.

In the rural areas of Northern New Brunswick, too, those of French mother tongue multiplied their numbers to a surprising extent, but never to a point at which they might control the destinies of their province; their opportunity has now passed and emigration or assimilation are the choices facing most young Acadians today.

This is the demographic setting for the "Maîtres chez nous" campaign. If English has clearly become the only language for advancement everywhere else on the continent, if French-Canadians are to be hemmed in by an almost insurmountable language barrier, then the full force of the legislature must be exerted to make French the preferred language inside Quebec, so that those who wish to retain the language of their grandfathers will continue to have at least one haven of refuge in North America.

This force is already being exerted in many ways. At the time that Shawinigan and the other private power companies were taken over by the province, it was openly proclaimed that one of the motives was to assure the ascendancy of the French language in this industry and among its many suppliers. When the Société Générale de Financement acquired Marine Industries, the president of this government-sponsored holding company stated that its new subsidiary would be "le plus puissant ensemble industriel contrôlé par des Canadiens français"*; the use of "Canadiens français" instead of "Québecois" underlines the extent to which the English-speaking minority has become a forgotten element in the new Quebec.

Thirty years ago, English was virtually the only language used in industry and commerce in the Province of Quebec. A knowledge of French was useful but certainly not essential: in the factories and elsewhere, the burden of bilinguality was on the French-Canadian workman rather than on the non-French foreman.

Today, the population of the cities of Quebec have become overwhelm-

*René Paré, as quoted in Le Devoir of August 27, 1965.

ingly French-speaking, everywhere except at Montreal, and the new citizens are not bothering to learn the second language to the same extent as did their predecessors. Outside Montreal, the 1961 Census found that 44% of the adult males in urban areas spoke "French Only" and the pressure is, therefore, toward hiring of personnel, at all levels, whose mother tongue is French.

This trend first became evident in such occupations as retail sales, where there is the most contact with the general population, but has now spread into other types of employment (wholesaling, public relations, etc.) where the personality and natural ability of the candidate are the important factors toward his hiring; those who prefer to work in English are, increasingly, finding it desirable to move to another province where they can make better use of their particular talents.

There is still ample opportunity in Quebec, however, for English-speaking professional men. Two centuries of education and experience cannot be acquired overnight and the educational system of Quebec Province has only recently been oriented toward production of engineers, managers and all those other categories in which non-French personnel will probably continue to predominate for several more decades. Even these latter, however, will probably tend to concentrate more and more at Montreal as the jobs elsewhere are taken over by graduates of the French-Canadian universities.

The ideal of "Maîtres chez nous" is a province in which only French need be spoken and where the French-Canadian can truly feel at home. For practical reasons, however, we shall probably see a compromise, with Montreal retaining a bilingual status; only by retaining English-speaking personnel in the metropolis will French-Canadians be available in sufficient numbers to take over the key jobs elsewhere and so make French the universal language of work everywhere except at Montreal.

Conclusions

The preceding chapters have traced the growth of the French-speaking population of Canada from a total of barely 80,000 persons in 1765 to over five million today. They have outlined the manner in which the outward spread of the French-speaking area, so remarkable during the 19th Century, came to a gradual halt during the present century.

They have shown, also, the extent to which assimilation is affecting the younger Canadians of French origin who live outside the Province of Quebec. The historical evidence presented indicates that two languages of unequal strength cannot co-exist in intimate contact and that the weaker must, inevitably, disappear.

Although French is still spoken in many homes outside the Soo-Moncton limits, the parents will usually be found to have spent their formative years in the geographical isolation of a predominantly-French rural community or in the psychological isolation of an urban enclave; such isolation is no longer possible in this day of television and teen-age mobility, and assimilation commences as soon as a threshold degree of contact with the stronger language has been attained.

Meanwhile, the English-speaking minority within Quebec is being weakened by heavy out-migration toward more congenial regions of the continent. This movement is certainly not new — the census figures show that it has existed for over a century — but it may well accelerate as the French language increases in power and prestige and as trained French-Canadians become available to displace the present non-French personnel in factories and elsewhere.

The forecast, therefore, emerges of a Canada in which the relative strengths of the two major language groups may remain similar to those found today but within which there will be a much more pronounced linguistic segregation: French within Quebec and English elsewhere.

Although Montreal may well retain its bilingual character, the English-speaking population of other parts of Quebec will probably decline in actual numbers, not merely in relative strength. Outside Quebec, French will continue to be spoken in the border counties of Ontario and New Brunswick but will virtually disappear from Southern Ontario, the Atlantic Region and the Western Provinces.

Such a forecast is, of course, based on the assumption that underlying conditions will not change greatly from those prevailing during the past few decades. It must be assumed that there will not be a serious economic slump in Quebec which would trigger a mass exodus of job-seekers and rejuvenate the French-speaking population of Southern Ontario. Also, we cannot foresee the extent to which proposed federal subsidization may succeed in prolonging the existence of French-speaking groups elsewhere, nor can we predict future trends in birthrates and immigration.

If this forecast is accurate, then our politicians and editors should commence now to prepare the public for the inevitable by showing that the disappearance of linguistic minorities is a natural phenomenon, rather than the consequence of some "genocidal" plot.

If the public is not so prepared, then the psychological shock when the minorities do disappear could be far more harmful to Canadian unity than will be the actual disappearance.

APPENDICES

Appendix A:

Definitions of Census Terms

Mother Tongue: In 1961, as in 1951 and 1941, this term was defined as "the language first learned in childhood and still understood. In the case of infants, the language commonly spoken in the home was recorded."

In 1931, however, a more rigorous definition had been used: "The language learned in childhood and still *spoken* by the person."

Ethnic Origin: In the census, a person's ethnic group is traced through his father, the 1961 question being: "To what ethnic or cultural group did you or your ancestor (on the male side) belong on coming to this continent?"

In 1941, persons of mixed (Indian and white) blood were classed as "Half-breed". This term disappeared in 1951 and such persons are now classed in the conventional manner, according to the origin of the father (unless they are living on a reserve, in which case they are classed as Indians).

Religion: The Census separates those in communion with Rome into "Roman Catholics" and "Ukrainian (Greek) Catholics"; the latter are not to be confused with "Greek Orthodox".

Rural and Urban: Prior to 1951, the urban population was defined as that residing in incorporated cities, towns and villages. In 1951, there was a reclassification, from urban to rural, of the residents of incorporated areas having a population of less than 1,000 (such "ghost towns" were particularly numerous in Saskatchewan and Quebec). Also in 1951, and again in 1956 and 1961, urban areas were progressively enlarged to include the unincorporated outskirts of many cities. Some caution must, therefore, be used when comparing the rural-urban figures taken from different censuses.

Accuracy of Enumeration: In general, census enumerators write down the answers given them, without attempting, for example, to authenticate an ethnic origin or to verify a person's claim to knowledge of a second language.

In certain parts of the country, this may have introduced a significant factor of error into the census results. It can be readily appreciated that not all citizens utilized the same criteria when deciding whether they were bilingual; more subtle was the error introduced when the person enumerated gave, as his ethnic origin, that corresponding to his father's language, rather than to the language of the first ancestor, on the male side, to come to this continent.

Appendix B:

Sources of Statistical Material

Figures used in this book have, unless otherwise specified, been obtained from publications of the Dominion Bureau of Statistics; the author would like to express his gratitude to the Ottawa Public Library for having made available a complete collection of census reports, dating back to 1851.

For the benefit of those who may wish to do further research, the exact source of each figure is listed below. For 1961, it is necessary to use the loose-leaf Census Bulletins ("CB" below); previous censuses are available as sets of bound volumes.

Where some manipulation of the published figures has been necessary, the calculation is shown. Comments will be found, where appropriate, as to the element of approximation entering into derived results.

Table	Source
1	CB 1.2-5, Table 37; CB 1.2-9, Table 66
2	CB 1.3-5, Tables 97 and 98
3	CB 7.1-9, Table 1
4	CB 1.3-5, Table 96 (20 years and over) 1951, Vol II, Table 19 1941, Vol. III, Table 38 1931, Vol. I, Table 46
5	CB 1.3-5, Table 97; calculation used was:

$$\text{Bilingual} = \frac{\text{M.T. French} - \text{French Only}}{\text{M.T. French}}$$

The error due to persons of non-French M.T. who speak "French Only" has been minimized through choice of cities in which the number of such persons is virtually negligible.

Table	Source
6	CB 1.2-5, Table 37
7	CB 1.2-9, Table 66

Table	Source
8	CB 1.2-9, Table 66 1951, Volume I, Table 56 1941, Volume II, Table 54 1911, Volume II, Table VIII; (actually, origin)
9	CB 1.3-2, Table 82 and CB 1.3-5, Table 96, give figures by provinces; figures for the border counties were obtained directly from D.B.S. $\text{App. Assim.} = \dfrac{\text{Eth. Fr.} - \text{M.T. Fr.}}{\text{Ethnic French}} \Bigg\}$ 0-4 age group
10	CB 1.2-5, Table 37; CB 1.2-9, Table 66
11	Figures for the various counties were obtained directly from D.B.S., those for the metro areas will be found in CB 1.3-2, Table 84 and CB 1.3-5, Table 98
12	CB 1.3-2, Table 82; CB 1.3-5, Table 96 (Apparent Assimilation calculated as in Table 9)
13	CB 1.3-2, Table 82; CB 1.3-5, Table 96 1951, Vol. II, Table 5; Vol. II, Table 22 1941, Vol. III, Table 11; Vol. III, Table 42 1931, Vol. I, Table 38; Vol. II, Table 58 (all ages) and Vol. IV, Table 58 (deduct)
14	CB 1.3-2, Table 82 and CB 1.3-5, Table 96
15	CB 1.3-5, Table 96 1951, Volume II, Table 22 1941, Volume III, Table 22 1931, Volume II, Table 58 less Vol. IV, Table 58
16	Figures for the border counties were obtained from D.B.S.
17	cf #15
18	CB 1.3-5, Table 96 A small error arises from the presence of some persons who speak "French Only" although their mother tongue is neither French nor English. The number of such persons in Ontario and New Brunswick would be quite small.

Table	Source
19	CB 1.3-5, Table 96 1941, Volume III, Table 42
20	CB 1.3-5, Table 96 1951, Volume II, Table 22 1941, Volume III, Table 42
21	CB 7.1-1, Table 2 and CB 1.2-8, Table 59
22	CB 1.3-2, Table 82 1951, Volume II, Table 5 1941, Volume III, Table 11 1931, Volume I, Table 38
23	CB 1.3-5, Table 95 1951, Volume II, Table 21 1941, Volume I, Table 45 1931, Volume I, Table 49
24	CB 1.3-11, Table 125
25	CB 1.3-11, Table 126
26	CB 1.3-10, Table 123 For each ethnic origin, the calculation was: $\text{Degree of Preference} = \frac{\text{M. T. English}}{\text{M. T. Engl.} + \text{M. T. French}}$
27	cf #23
28	cf #23
29	CB 1.2-7, Table 48 (for 1901-1961, incl.) 1871, Volume I, Table IV
30	CB 1.2-8, Table 58 In Chapter X, circulation figures quoted are A.B.C., in most cases, and were obtained from Ayer's Directory
31	United States Census figures
32	These figures were obtained from a very interesting historical review, found on pages 133-153 of Volume 1 of the 1931 Census.
33	CB 1.2-9, Tables 64 and 66

Table	Source
34	CB 1.3-5, Table 96 1951, Volume II, Table 22 1941, Volume III, Table 42 1931, Volume II, Table 58 less Volume IV, Table 58
35	CB 1.2-9, Table 66 1871, Volume I, Table III (actually, origin) Note: Here, as in other places, ethnic origin has had to be used for the earlier years due to unavailability of M. T. figures.
36	CB 1.2-9, Table 64 1951, Volume I, Table 55 1941, Volume I, Table 44 for 1881 and 1901, see: 1941, Volume I, Table 33
37	CB 7.1-1, Table 1 (for 1901 to 1961, incl.) 1871, Volume I, Table I
38	1951, Volume II, Table 52
39	CB 1.3-2, Table 82 1951, Volume II, Table 5 1941, Volume III, Table 11
40	CB 1.2-7, Table 49 for 1871-1931, see: 1941, Volume I, Table 21 1851, Volume I, Tables 1 and 3
41	CB 1.2-9, Table 64 1931, Volume II, Table 58 for 1871 and 1901, see: 1941, Volume I, Table 33 for 1837, see: 1931, Volume I, page 149
42	calculated from the figures of the previous table
43	CB 1.2-9, Table 65 and Table 68 1931, Volume II, Table 58 for 1871 and 1901, see: 1931, Volume I, Table 35 Note: in 1961, Metropolitan Montreal earlier years, Montreal Island
44	CB 1.3-6, Table 99 1951, Volume II, Table 25 1941, Volume III, Table 45 1931, Volume I, Table 72

Table	Source
45	cf #43
46	CB 1.2-5, Table 35 1951, Volume I, Table 32 for 1871-1901, see: 1941, Volume I, Table 33
47	CB 1.2-5, Table 36 for 1871-1941, see: 1941, Volume I, Table 33
48	CB 1.2-5, Table 37 1871, Volume I, Table III
49	CB 1.2-5, Table 37 1931, Volume II, Table 32 1901, Volume I, Table XI 1871, Volume I, Table III
50	cf #49
51	cf #49
52	cf #49; also: 1951, Volume I, Table 34
53	CB CT-4 "Population by census tracts"
54	CB 1.2-9, Table 68 1951, Volume I, Table 58 1941, Volume II, Table 54 1901, Volume I, Table XI } These are by origins 1871, Volume I, Table III }
55	CB 1.2-5, Tables 35 and 39 1951, Volume I, Tables 32 and 36 1941, Volume I, Table 33; Volume II, Table 31 1931, Volume I, Table 35; Volume II, Table 32 1901, Volume I, Table XI
56	CB 1.2-7, Table 52
57	CB 1.3-5, Table 98 (20 years and over)
58	CB CT-13 "Population by census tracts"

Table	Source
59	CB 1.2-9, Table 67 1941, Volume IV, Table 15 1921, Volume I, Table 28 1901, Volume I, Table XI 1871, Volume I, Table III
60	CB 1.2-9, Table 67; CB 1.2-6, Table 45 1951, Volume I, Table 57 and Volume I, Table 42 1941, Volume IV, Table 15 and Volume II, Table 40 1911, Volume II, Tables XIV & IV
61	CB 1.2-9, Table 68 1951, Volume I, Table 58 1941, Volume II, Table 55 1901, Volume I, Table XI (added from sub-areas)
62	CB 1.2-9, Table 66 1951, Volume I, Table 56 1941, Volume II, Table 54 1901, Volume I, Table XI (origin) 1871, Volume I, Table III (origin)
63	cf #62
64	CB 1.2-5, Table 37 1951, Volume I, Table 34 for 1871-1931, cf #62
65	for 1941-1961, cf #62 1911, Volume II, Table VIII
66	CB 1.2-5, Table 37 and CB 1.2-9, Table 66 1951, Volume I, Table 34 and Volume I, Table 56 1941, Volume II, Table 31 and Volume II, Table 54
67	CB 1.2-7, Table 49 1951, Volume I, Table 45 1871-1941 all shown in: 1941, Volume I, Table 21
68	cf #69
69	CB 1.2-9, Table 64 1951, Volume I, Table 55 1941, Volume I, Table 44 (also shows 1931 figures) 1901, Volume I, Table XI (origin)